Sound of the Sacred Beads

A Poet's Journey into India

PROSE & POETRY
BY
SUSAN KLAUBER

Sandtrove Press
Fairfield, Iowa, USA

Sound of the Sacred Beads
A Poet's Journey into India

Copyright © 2010 by Susan Klauber

All rights reserved. No part of this book may be used or reproduced in any manner whatsoever without written permission, except in the case of brief quotations embodied in critical articles and reviews. For information contact:

Sandtrove Press
Fairfield, Iowa
sandtrovepress@gmail.com

Cover Photo: Joe Stanski
                  Crystal *Sri Chakra* surrounded by sacred
                  Navaratna beads.

Cover and Interior Design: Marty Hulsebos

Author Photo: Marty Hulsebos

Interior Photos: Karl Grobl (©Karlgrobl.com pgs. 22, 86, 132)
                      Marty Hulsebos (pgs. 1, 33, 34/35, 63, 98, 128, 131)
                      Erik Vigmostad (pgs. 13, 69, 100, 119, 156)
                      Sw. Vijayeswarananda (pg. 133)
                      Powell Woods (pgs. 64, 65, 104)

First Edition 2010
Library of Congress Control Number: 2010904121
Soft Cover ISBN: 978-0-9845139-0-1
Printed in the United States of America.

Dedication

To Mother and Father

Thank you for the opportunity to travel and the wisdom to at least try to appreciate the importance of the inner silence in fulfilling our stay here on earth.

Why India?

*It takes time
to hear the details
of a sincere question
collecting under the sane
rehearsals of every day,
if only an instant
to hear the answer.*

*Stories of saints and holy places
still circle the globe
calling collect
to whoever wants
to accept.*

Acknowledgements

I want to thank the editors of the following journals and anthologies for previously publishing some of the poems:

Eclipsed Moon Coins "Stolen Shoes"
The MacGuffin "Western Trash Man"
Poetry Motel (Sidebar Edition) "Where Silence Meets"

Special thanks to Diane Frank and Rustin Larson for their advice and inspiration in writing the poems, to Walt Collett for his input, and to the writers in Diane's and Rustin's workshops for their suggestions. Appreciation also goes to Marty Hulsebos for the cover and interior design, Joe Stanski for the original cover photo, Care Connet for editing and proofreading, Pundit Sarathi for his help with the glossary, and Devorah McKay, Allan Cobb, and many others for their help and encouragement. My gratitude goes to the photographers who so graciously allowed me to use their photos inside the book: Karl Grobl, Marty Hulsebos, Erik Vigmostad, Sw. Vijayeswarananda, and Powell Woods. And to my beloved husband and travel-mate Bob, thank you for arranging our first trip to India. I was hooked after that.

Contents

I
"Most welcome. Which country are you coming?"

Western Porcelain Goddess in the Holy Valley of the Gods	3
The Freak	5
Twelve Time Zones the Other Side of Order	7
Western Trash Man	8
Dhanyavad	9
English?	10
Signs of India	12
Traveling Backwards	14
The Thread in the *Mala*	15
Dog Exchange	17
Indian Persona	18
Between the *Japa* Beads: Six Minutes	20
Delhi *Darshan*	21
Escape to Oberoi	23
Smells of India	24
Breaking Through the Trade Barrier	25
The Hindu Auctioneer	27
In the 7-11 Store of the Gods	29
Hybrid Love Affair	31

II
"Hello Auntie"

Ahimsa	37
Pearls Culture Peacefulness	38
Cross-Cultural Lightning	39
The Silk Sell	40
Bull	42
Golfing in Vedaland	44
Kovalam Beach	46
In the Vernacular	47
Women Don't Wear Bathing Suits in India	48
Lamani Woman, Carried on the Wind	49

Where Silence Meets	50
It's a Girl	51
Air Walk	52
Sisters of the Ashram	53
Scooter	54
The Americanization of *Lila*	55
Pink Coral for *Lila*	56
Faces in the Suburbs	57
Stolen Shoes	61

III
IMPRESSIONS IN THE INTERIOR

Parade of the Pilgrims	67
Headwaters of the *Ganga*	69
Ganga Devi	71
Kunja Devi	72
The Goddess Wears Crystal	73
Mother God	74
Scupltor of Belur	75
On the Road to Tirupathi	77
The Outing from the Old Ladies' Home	79
Tirupathi Tirumala Temple	81
Beggars Outside the Temple	85
Weight of the Beads	87
Pradakshina	88
Coral Beads Dropped on the Pavement	90
After the Fall (Picking up the Beads)	91
Shore Temple	92
Rameshwaram	93
In the Palm of Madurai	96

IV
BEYOND THE TRANSITORY

God Wore Sandals	101
Nakshatra's Ride	102
Mataji	103
For the Love of Mother	105

"The Hum of Creation Comes from the Slightest Stir of Mother Divine's Feet"	106
Sanatana Dharma	107
Wearer of the Beads	109
Christmas Morning with *Baba*	111
Giver of the Beads	112
Christmas Night with Divine Mother	114
Seeing a Miracle?	116
Just to be with Mother	117
Learning to Bead the Sounds of Nature	118
Suburban Monkey	119
Three Meditations: Trinity of Beads	121
Dwellers in the Caves	125
Memo to God	127
In the Center of the Beads	128
Reflection from a Hammock by the Bay of Bengal	129
Into the Fire	129
Guesswork?	130

V
FLIGHT HOME

Meera	135
Flight Home	136
India	137
Transcendental Transformer	138
Lessons from India	140
India in Translation	141
Epilogue	143

GLOSSARY	144
PARTING NOTES TO THE TRAVELER	156
ABOUT THE AUTHOR	159

Western Porcelain Goddess in the Holy Valley of the Gods

"Cold Thirsts and Hot Sips" is the menu title in a Rishikesh restaurant: three cement walls, open air, fifty meters from the Ganges, almost blue, rushing. A dead body catches half way across, under the wooden footbridge. Dark yellow marigolds float in a garland, past the billboard, "Holy Valley of the Gods."

I am five dusty taxi hours up the Himalayan foothills from my first glimpse of India, the upper right half of an airport quadrangle barricaded by a row of brown faces startling me with their black eyes. White specks of eyeballs are set in a line, five foot four inches even, staring, still as the brown and gray of the sweaters. The next imprint is the taste of diesel fumes that never disappear, even as the taxi rolls further from our thirty-hour jumbo adventure that somewhere over the Atlantic stalled at the cruising speed of a windowless prison term. My lungs burn to breathe, never to escape Delhi.

The hotel is a dark, side-street bungalow: two a.m. sleepy night watchman, basic bed-and-chair room with attached bath and toilet paper that I soon learn is luxury. A half-inch thick roll of Goody toilet tissue is one-tenth the cost of most rooms that double in price for a western porcelain goddess.

We sleep through to the still dark morning and the distant call of a lone male voice chanting to God. I'm not sure which God he calls by the strange warbles of unfamiliar words, but I can hear the spaces of silence where I have talked to Christ and imagined Buddha sitting inside me transforming midnight into May.

A dog barks through the silence, then a radio and the neighbor's husband hacking, then spitting: gut-trenching mucous splatches that become so familiar to the Indian morning I assume they must be a learned response passed on from father to son, like the chanting of God's names, to clear the day of any residue from last night's incomplete dreams.

I learn to rise earlier to hear my prayers, before the clatter of too many people takes hold: a swarm of flesh and traffic layered into the atmosphere. I learn to breathe its unctuous human skin, learn to accept the smell of urine with sandalwood and the acidic constriction of diesel crowding me into an auto rickshaw. These metal rigs on wheels look like moving outhouses, and ride like a Tilt-a-Whirl cage on a motorcycle skimming eye level to the door handles speeding by on the cars.

Six rickshaws can squeeze into the space of two Ford Broncos, so for rush hour, rickshaws are the preferred choice of travel. And since Indians are five feet tall and one hundred pounds, a whole family, and even a stranger or two, can jam-pile into two seats. They nestle up beside us but don't smile, so we carry on breathing between the jousting of countless horns, honking and blaring so insistently that they blot out the conscious mind. The driver surrenders to a state of calm automation never witnessed inside a New York cabby's brain.

We trust him because the only thing left in chaos is instinct. Or maybe it's the familiarity of age, like the cars, white Ambassador taxis, rounded from the 1950's, the memory of leather and chrome that I want to touch, high cushiony seats that let us see over the hood.

The brown or gray sweater of the driver crumples, like it was when he woke up in it fifteen hours before, and like he'll sleep in it, in the back seat of his car, after he drives us late into the night, where a loud horn suddenly stretches one-and-a-half lanes into two multicolored trucks with our Ambassador squeezed in between. We go in opposite directions but somehow the same, like the billboards that twist English to a new level of "men's suitings" and "hotels of homely comfort," or like the newspaper that recounts last year's election as the "throwing up of the president."

We wind by wood shacks and cement block homes like we saw in South America or *National Geographic*. Apples pile into pyramids stacked on rickety wooden carts pressed against the only available road.

We land in a restaurant twelve thousand miles from home and carefully select the safe items from the menu. I wipe my fork clean, eyes wide with the smell of ginger and hot pepper burning a hole into my heart, beside the road sign that reads, "Slow Down, Enjoy My Curves."

The Freak

Rishikesh, India: home of saints and hippies.
A bank queue: long and traditional,
bureaucratic boring through smudged air.
Trapped and forgotten:
conversation granted, as sanity preserver.

When he was nine, he was abducted by light beings and shown manuscripts in a universal language encrypted under his left breast, below the long brown hair and weed-cured eyes. They smile at me, deja-vu, thirty years ago when I scouted the world for windstorms, adrenaline wings to hurl me through the TV, past the weekly shopping carts and checkbooks, balancing matter with what matters.

He was taken to Patal Bhuwaneshwar where Himalayan peaks bolt into the clouds, thousands of feet above human heads. Star beings first landed there and seeded the earth like computer chips implanted in our genes: some from the Pleiades and some from Orion, with some of us thinking we're from Canada or America.

Passports are necessary to change money. It takes extra time in India to find out we are all immigrants from the stars that landed at the border of India and Tibet. There's a cave still there, seven levels deep, current residence of the one hundred and eight God forms we humans imagined somewhere in our closed eyes, wandering the cosmic frontier.

He was shown inside the heart of the mountain: shafts of light, all the Gods, Hopi Indians, Australian aborigines, every knowledge once known, preserved intact. His guru Sai Baba still lives there, and bi-locates to south India where thousands swear they see him every day. He is sure Baba blessed his mission, and revealed seven manuscripts to him in the caves to communicate to the world.

We are like slaves or animals, three-dimensional humans in a universe of five- and higher-dimensional star forms with ten DNA to our two.

The line shortens to him and me.

Alien grays and whites abduct humans to reclaim our lost DNA.

My signature works slowly, two dimensions imprinted into American

Express.

Read about it in *Turn off the TV*, to be written soon.

Eight dimensions are left in my brain,
parting slowly down the dirt road to Rishikesh.

Twelve Time Zones the Other Side of Order

It's jet-lag blues: glazed eyes cave like a barmaid hag, the entire earth weighted into my brain waves, reducing planetary motion to a gravitational slug. This is my perfect entry to India, twelve time zones the other side of order, where it takes an hour to find a postcard and the rest of the day to buy the stamp.

Indian directions understate. "Five-minutes walk straight along" clings for twenty minutes, dripping my sweat, skin, and T-shirt into a limping lump. The central post office greets me like a row of jailhouse inmates. Twenty-six barred counter windows, guarded by untranslatable signs, stare down lineups of bodies decomposing in crooked queues that reveal their fake identity only after fifteen minutes of waiting.

Mutating from one germy cell to the other repeats for several karma-purging incarnations until the proper stamp is secured, pasted securely in its corner, and then diligently scrutinized before the official rubber stamp mashes the face of Gandhi into the worn-out wooden counter. Then it's silent prayer time, as with everything in India. I invoke divine help for the card to reach its final destination.

With blessings, it arrives in two weeks in America, where a friend reads it in thirty-seven seconds and never comprehends the lifetime of patience worked out of my pores, squeezed and depleted of all western slick, leaving me an airless vacuum sucking on hope.

Indian atmosphere is thin chaos, diesel breathing with no tension, no pressurized pen filling a day planner. Street signs? Rare sightings. Address numbers on buildings? Extinct or indistinct, roadmaps yet unborn. This is a land of promise for civil engineers, accountants, computer specialists, not cartographers. Maps are unthinkable for things that have remained where they are longer than human imagination.

The Brahma cows know. They sit it out, hunched by the road, and rise only occasionally for a lazy amble through speeding stockpiles of scooters and auto rickshaws.

My mind, divested of chatter, long ago wiped into the void of twelve time zones, slumps on the udder side of Brahma, pavement smells pressed with the ink stamped into my eye-slits, "Return to sender, addressee unknown."

Western Trash Man

My American engineer husband burns to put trash barrels all over India, start an immediate ad campaign to change five thousand years of Brahma cows chewing the vegetarian road kill from human hands. Rice and *dahl*, served on last century's digestible palm leaf, disgorge into today's rickety dirt streets on inedible plastic bags and laminated white cartons haloed from blue chip America's scientific genius.

If one more boon were granted his elegant sub-particle mind, it would be a bounty on all the temple loudspeakers screaming scratchy Indian names of God. Like neuro-surgical needles jammed into the eardrum, they pierce and shriek, as unconscionably deafening as the rusty switchblades of political hucksters screeching the streets for a new rightwing-leftwing coalition for zanity.

After two days of jostling the city streets with the noise-trash density of nine hundred million Indians jack-hammering the tidy Iowa plains of his bones, he starts wearing ear-blockers, industrial strength, imported from his U.S. lab.

He carries the chocolate wrapper, thoughtfully, for three hours, then silently drops it in the streets.

DHANYAVAD

Dhanyavad is a modern Hindi word for thank you. But in India, nothing new seems to stick. Pink and blue paint cracks and crumbles, returning to the original gray of cinder houses. They don't want to stick around either, gaping holes in the cement façade for the breath of air that Mother first formed into *Bharat's* skin.

That was a time when hands were created for giving; no other expectation was necessary. Now, it stirs a gentle nodding of the Indian head, somewhere between a "yes" and a "no," confusing my logical western black or white into a "maybe." I watch Indian eyes murmur side to side, in agreeable communion with inner assumptions. But I don't know. I extend money to a corner vendor for water; he takes it methodically and places it in a drawer. A beggar withdraws her freshly rupeed hand from mine, and moves on. Their faces do not stir.

I like to hear a thank you or see a smile, but the silence penetrates deeper than a rejected kiss. I listen to my mind talking in intimate detail, determining who should be doing what to whom, as though the universe just formed and the rules of politeness are still being worked out. I hear *Bharat's* ancient code whisper under the vacant imprint of the kiss, "No need to thank someone for something that is their duty to perform."

Gifts to beggars, duty? Payments to vendors, duty? Novel concepts for my capitalist mind accustomed to a boss's gratuitous smile, placed eye level on a job applicant punching alphabets into a machine so she can pay for whole wheat pasta and Pop-tarts.

In India the applicant waits, unthanked, in the silence of a rickshaw driver maneuvering his quiet path through the reckless clutter of scooters, dogs, cars and cows, trucks, bullock carts, bicycles and people. Smiling musical chairs have fallen away long ago.

ENGLISH?

The sign over the doorway reads, "Hotel." We climb up the narrow stairs that end in a room full of tables and chattering Indians, with waiters hustling platters of the daily special.

"What is the cost of your rooms?"

The money taker sitting at the entrance looks at us without a smile. "Rooms no, sir. Hotel."

"This is a hotel, yes?"

"Yes, sir, hotel. Rooms no. Only hotel." His hand gestures toward the rows of worn wooden tables as if to say, *Can't you see it's only a hotel?* Indians hunched over stainless steel plates do not look up, too busy scooping mounds of rice and *dahl* into their mouths with their bare hands.

The stairs seem longer and quieter on the way down, our brains still upstairs wondering what just transpired.

At a "real" hotel we are given two options. After looking at both rooms to ensure that the fingerprints on the walls do not extend to the linen, and that the aftershock of street noise is within human decibel range, we return to the desk clerk.

"We'll take room two oh three, please."

"Only one room, sir."

"Yes, we'll take two oh three, please."

"Which one, sir?"

I try speaking the words more slowly than my husband. "Room, number, two, oh, three."

The clerk looks at us quietly and glances down, withdrawing his confidence into a humble embarrassment. "You choose, madam."

I point in the general direction of the room. "The non-AC room."

Smiling relief, he turns to the boy and directs him to take us to room "two hundred and three."

Dialogue with Destiny (Behind Closed Doors)

I come to India with abstract, esoteric, and comprehensive thoughts compelling me to see more in life than the obvious. India confronts me with the very words I assume are a starting point, reduces them to the crematorium, and leaves me in the quiet void of human beings standing face to face, bags empty, packaging unnecessary.

Signs of India

> *Italics indicate actual spelling and words seen on Indian road signs, newspapers and billboards.*

Shus Repers stares at me like a crooked shingle flapping in the breeze over a ghost town. Its meaning vanishes in the empty space between what I know is English, and what someone long ago must have scrawled on the wooden boards of a street vendor's stall as a coded message for help. I imagine the Grim Reaper lopping off the heads of the Shus family before I remember I am in India, and this is a legitimate English sign informing me what the vendor is selling. The headline in the *Hindu Times* flashes in my memory, *Congress Hit by Drain Brain.*

My mind transfixes on sleuthing the real meaning. Perhaps *The Genius Gallary* store across the street can help. Stepping into the traffic, I slip on mushy slop of watermelon remnants, right next to a flap of wet dung and a trash hole big enough to rip the thong of my sandals. This leaves me right-barefooted and heading for the *Ding Dong Footwear* sign that boldly challenges my rigid, pseudo-European sophistication with the assurance it must be O.K. to wear dinner bells on my feet. Four lanes of traffic are only wide enough to allow for a nervous compromise, a pair of brass bells like the temple pundits ring to announce holy moments. The store is closed for lunch, 1:30 to 5!

I settle for a barefoot Indian spiced tea at *Café Mischief* and wonder why they have to ask you to *Eat All the Food You Buy Here.* Maybe *rostid chiken* is the mischief of genetically engineered roosters, and my choice of vegetarianism is wise. Hesitating to order before knowing what *chats* and *finger chips* are, I attempt an inquiry. After an incomprehensible translation, my snack of French fries arrives, coated with red-hot chili pepper!

Totally spice-jeeped, I wonder if *Drive-In Tyre Refittments* would be a safer choice for my feet, like the Michelin baby safely riding in the hubcap space of a rubber retread. Words of a Himalayan road sign whisper in my subconscious, *Don't Zoom to the Doom. Better Belate Than Never.*

I ponder my feet, and like every woman in a crisis of doubt, I sidestep into the *She's Collections* to check on the latest fashions. If nothing nice grabs me here, there is always the option next door, *Smiling Gifts For Your Home*. I've always wanted a happy rug that snaps one-liners every time anyone steps on the short circuit hidden in the fruit salad pattern! I decide shopping barefoot is fun and look forward to getting exhausted, then returning to my *Hotel with Homely Comfort* to relax in my *Cheep Room*, fully satisfied with my *Worthful Spending*.

Cosmic inspirations always reward with enlightenment. As I step into a rickshaw painted *We Two Ours One*, my heart fills with a dense sense of community. We pass by a road sign, *No Race. No Rally. Enjoy Splendour of Valley*, assuring me we are in the zone. The driver gently follows the guidance of the angel car ahead, *Powar Brake Keep Distence*, then smooths into *The Ease Zone* rest stop past the Highway Department advisory, *If You Love Her, Divorce Speed*.

In the faultless radiance of true love, I believe India has succumbed to *Treasure Cleanliness*, until I step my bare foot out of the rickshaw and into a squish of unidentifiable mush. Enlightenment bolts in a squidgy flash. I know where I can have my shooz repaired!

Traveling Backwards

I travel all the way from Bangalore to Chennai backward, our train seats offering me no option but a reverse view of the passage of time spreading over the flat farm fields. I do not worry, because I assume the return trip will correct my displaced orientation, face me forward once again, and allow me to recapture the lost dimension.

But I am wrong. The train from Chennai to Bangalore is an equally backward cascade. Coconut palms and rice paddies stream into the back of my head, through my brain, then shoot out my eyeballs into the future that I remember having left, but that still stares at me in the solitary horizon.

A lone human body, displacing the monotony of farmland, peaks above the drying fields, as though the day is unfolding its normal sequence. To this sari-clad sentinel, the train speeds past. But I can still see her, caught in the future, the day stopped in the same spot of land she tilled yesterday, and the day before, and the day before that. We do not leave each other, because we never meet.

I wonder whether any trains in India travel forward. My original train from Bangalore to Chennai must have kept on going, past Chennai into the Bay of Bengal. It circled the globe forever backward and reappeared in Mumbai to repeat its journey across south India, picking up every spiritual traveler in Bangalore and taking us back to Chennai.

The return voyage is only a mirage train that cycles in the opposite direction, circling the globe equally backwards. I never really leave, so I never return. I just am, and India just is, traveling east and west but never really going anywhere.

I am left with my existence and one last nagging option, that maybe my going is the mirage train, and this one is real. I am a Zen koan without inspiration or expiration, just a pen scribbling on a piece of paper. This is India.

The Thread in the *Mala*

What holds this crazy, chaotic place together? In even the smallest dots on the map of India, we are pummeled by noise, dirt, and people everywhere. Not just the usual walk-and-talk traffic of individuals going and coming, but everyday life spills into the streets with the closeness of a campground. Open windows and doors of eternal summer are like thin walls of tents, unable to contain the neighbor's rasping cough, the smell of breakfast frying on the pan, the pop tunes of radio stars and the parent scolding the teenager. Burps and farts of family familiarity pour into public airways with the Indian nonchalance of a child embodied in the soul of a grandmother.

I begin to almost marvel. Under the chaotic chatter of horns and people and moving parts of life's noisy undoing, something seems to work. Life here flows. Uptight? Rush around to an appointment? Open the store on time? Rare indeed. Only a truly westernized materialist of an Indian would throw such jarring tantrums into the sound waves. Even the poorest man sleeps soundly, stretched out on the curb under the shade of a tree for afternoon nap. There's a peaceful sensibility, a guileless given, as if the beads of individuality are held together by an invisible thread. A feeling of tolerance slips along under the illogical sequences of material inefficiency.

I wonder if this benign acceptance happens as a defense mechanism against the morass of bureaucracy entrenched in the society. But I realize that there is something deeper going on, because this wouldn't happen to hundreds of millions of people all at once, with no shotguns forcing the issue. Filtering through my menu of harmonizing influences, I deduce that one unique mainstay of Indian life is the Vedic chanting. These sounds of eternity have been repeated over and over again, passed on generation to generation for so long, that the sound has become a collective memory stored in the genes. It moves through the soil. The skin bordering one body merges into the next in an underlying acceptance, a flow of air so subtle it is sacred *soma*, what I remember Maharishi called the glue of the universe. Indians move along different paths, sometimes breaking into political and religious schisms with the fierceness of demons. Yet under it all, the *soma* flows, the invisible string melding the material with the spiritual.

Indians know it intuitively: the glow in the brown skin, the capacity to move, to do, to act without feeling strained; the ability to look at someone without judgment, to simply share the humanness.

I wonder what Canada, America or Europe would be like if we merged our efficiency and economic freedom with the simple sound of eternity, if we married the bustle of material got-to-do's with the spiritual center of just being.

And what would India be like if it molded its crash course in western economics into its spiritual heritage, freed its own citizens to become sages? Would it be able to turn ancient Vedic wisdom into an elegant solution for liberating the world from the deteriorated human values of western materialism? India of the future, a model for the balance of spirit and material progress? Dare I dream?

Dog Exchange

Maybe we should take all the dogs from America on a cultural exchange, let them loose in the streets of India.

In America it's difficult to walk the streets without chain fencing as the only protection from hostile fangs. The owner's prize magnum waits, warming death in the deeper-throated gnarls. My memory of being chased by two barking froth-jowled monsters, tears wind-shearing down my seven-year-old cheeks, is as pungent with dog panic as the open jaws and fifty-four fangs of the trained attack dog that broke his chain and leaped for my throat twenty years later. They imbed as cruelly as the foot-long needle stabbed daily into my stomach after a rabid black mongrel bit my leg.

In India I avoid eye contact with the first runty stray I see slinking the gutter. His ribs stick out in the memory of a starved wolf. He glances up, then passes by me invisible, his head returning to the street, paws continuing their cadence like four old ladies singing hymns. It never gets more exciting than that, countless dogs later.

Maybe Indians tranquilize canines like we spay them. Or maybe they slip hashish into their *dahl* bowls, so the fur doesn't grow wild. Dogs lie in the street, contented lumps of skin merged with earth, perpendicular to America.

Indian Persona

They don't seem to have a persona I am familiar with, the front guard around the heart.

I get used to their curiosity. Eyes stare at me like a child gaping at the new kid on the block, no attempt to hide the focus. No edge of judgment separates us. No glare of distrust burns the subconscious airwaves. The interchange is more like water pouring into water. The surface swirls and bubbles for a moment of temporary displacement, then settles as the two waters merge, indistinguishable from each other. Eyes are simply benign channels for the flow of awareness from their being to mine, their open heart an essential force in the package of human interaction. It is impossible for me to feel threatened by innocence.

School children run to us as though we are their new adventure movie just released from fantasyland. They practice the first English words they learned at school, extracting each syllable from their long lost treasure. Each word punctuates the air, slowly, with exactly the same tone, the absence of cadence like a finger forgetting why it was pointed. "What. Is. Your. Name." They delight in trying to repeat "Susan" or "Bob," the unusual sounds rolled in their tongues like precious jewels added to their hidden treasure. They vibrate their new story in the secret world of foreign magic, then run off.

In the suburbs and smaller cities, adults watch as we pass by. Some rush up to us, eager to make friends, to tell us they have a son in New Jersey or an uncle in California, or simply to talk. Questions spill out like popping corn jettisoned into the air in all directions. "Where you from? You like India? The food? What is your profession? And you madam? How many children you have?"

Their cheery faces slump in sympathy, or pan numbly, unable to compute when we say we have no children. They smile approvingly when we say we are interested in India's spiritual heritage. Transcendental Meditation and Maharishi Mahesh Yogi draw a blank, unless they have seen him on cable TV. "Yes, yes, Maharishi-ji."

No subject seems taboo. "What is your salary?" slithers through the air like a giant eel, bending as easily around the cost of our plane ticket as the effect of the food on our regularity. "I want visit America. What is your address?"

The first time the subject of salary and money comes up, I sense the alarms go off in my mind. Money and home addresses are not on the savvy traveler's share list for the first few minutes of conversation. A rapid-fire takeover by a stranger comes as a mixed bag of humorous delight and caution. Can anyone be this cheerful and curious without a pocket to pick or a setup for fleecing?

I get used to the South Indian candor and the boundless energy in speaking to us. I am embarrassed by the speed with which I put up my defensive guard and suspect their motives so quickly. I revisit the boundaries I carry with me, relearning my codes of safe conduct, this time within the reach of my heart.

I wonder if this Indian candor with us is what happens when so many people live together on a daily basis. Or is it a vestige of their spiritual and cultural past? The ancient *rishis* taught them to see all people as family. Humanity is a superfluid vat of interchanging molecules, atoms, and ideas, with each person a letter of the cosmic alphabet floating in the broth. Skin is not a rigid boundary of individuality, but more a permeable passageway for the transfusion of sweat, air, water, and all the same elements that make up every human being. The coating over the heart is shed.

I check my spiritual bankbook and have to admit that simple innocence, like that in my quiet meditation, does not spread out to strangers, to strange lands. What makes anything strange anyway?

What would I be like if I never had the boundary of separateness cast its fear into my awareness, if I could truly open in trust, live the truth behind differences, "safe" in the hands of God?

Is it possible that the wisdom of the ancient *rishis* that I have sought for years comes down to the state of my heart?

Between the *Japa* Beads: Six Minutes

> *Japa is the repetition of a mantra aloud using sacred beads as a counter, as with a rosary.*

We can exist like computer monitors
flashing messages on and off,
professional programs designated to stop
at the first non-linear answer
or the first open-ended question,
our spirit secured with white western glue
bound in leather logic.

But can we sit one minute without thinking,
circling the moon,
listening silently under the cluttered rattle
of too many buses changing gears?

India sits six minutes,
like hands paused between *japa* beads.
Stray dogs lie in the road,
limp as wet towels laid out for drying.
Buses steer around them.

No shouts, no invectives to demonic gods,
"Kill the beast!"
Only the buses' mongrel groans
muffle under the bark of horns
growling through the soot.

In India I shed my whiteness quickly,
but I don't notice it happening,
like the dog resting, undisturbed,
under the guardian eyes of the moon.

Delhi *Darshan*

Wrinkled soiled hand taps my shoulder, cups palm up for U.S. *darshan*, "Ma, ma." Three rupees move from my wallet to her hand, both made of brown leather. They hang like animal hide to dry in the still air between two dark eyes I do not look into, and the non-existent smile I have stopped looking for.

I carry an empty molecule along the inner edge of my personality, swallowed inside a silken silence left after the dirty hand and my dismay collapse. Beyond reflex, beyond my tightened skin and the smell of unwashed body stains, past the vacant hole in my heart, I walk in a bottomless stillness far into mud-caked alleys of bent knees on barefoot sandals.

The war of repulsion and compassion stills in the communion of survival. Some beggars, old and thankless, stretch palms out when I pass. Others, weighed with dirty babies, wait where they have always waited, one hundred and eight incarnations too many, haunting inseparable from the tacky storefronts.

Batik pant-legs flap silently over wooden *Buddhas* and black-iron dancing *Shivas*. They cram the sidewalk, squeezing me zigzag through cluttered tables of holy and plastic beads, silver bell anklets, garish saris hanging in dark doorways like red-light street walkers. "Come in. I give you good price. Best quality goods," echoes through a shiny jungle of stainless pots and pans, stacked like tentacles of gigantic silver pears, bending and reaching for the only space available, skyward. I am afraid to look up, or risk stepping on the Brahma cow's last lunch.

I cramp and jostle with the heat of hundreds of bodies swerving into bicycles and rickshaws, plastic trash and fermenting leftovers. We all blow out of control in a clattered clatter of tin horns. "You like? Come, more inside," prods us as if we were slabs of dead meat stabbed for signs of blood. "Ma, ma." A finger jabs me. "Mother, mother." I bruise. The apples and oranges stay perfectly arranged, stoic pyramids suspended in front of two steady eyes.

"Buy me. Buy me. Give me. Give me," shatters my brain before I can hear the shock-wave coming, before I know I have to escape, closeted in a second floor no-star hotel, the smell of mold and money pressed onto my numbed skin. But I have to go back again and rumble through Parganya's marriage of business and despair, just to remember what it feels like, to hear India's barrage of human survival silence me, walking my body without a face.

Through the Sound of the Beading

I tell my friend I am trying to come to terms with the beggars, the poverty.

She stares at me, motionless. "One can never come to terms with it."

Escape to Oberoi

At the Oberoi, mahogany tables cloaked in white linen glitter sterling silver daggers guarded by crystal flutes. Triangular white napkins stand at attention, clean, ironed and starched, groomed by Puritan standards flown in fresh to Bangalore and Delhi. Five stars means orchid garden café under banyan boughs for breakfast, air-con and chandeliers for forty-entrée lunch, and Mozart wine after high tea while we snuff silver, slowly, into our blue veins.

We wear our cleanest T-shirts, pressed. Stagecoaches remain outside with the diesel smog and beggars in the street cluttered like Dickens' black alleys. Wealth puffs the polite chest only enough to be visible by eyes slanted to the proper degree. Shined to match the crystal, to see essences of Plato glowing under our otherwise common skin, we pierce past the vinyl rickshaw, by the doorman turbaned as a sultan guard.

One hundred fresh yellow gladiolas, five feet high, in a massive Ming vase centerpiece, reflect on twenty feet of polished ebony. Beyond the pressed soot and sweated air: off-white and gold marble, glass vistas to tropical gardens. Beyond the thick walls of nameless bodies crisscrossing trash crowded into overcrowded India: gourmet delicacies; the trickle of a fountain, rippling, just long enough to hear our breathing; the scent of honeysuckle slipping into our skin.

The muted voices of uniformed footmen whisper, just long enough, before the cleansing becomes antiseptic, before gold chains cling to our pores like roses at a funeral home, before we forget why we traveled as far as India in the first place.

SMELLS OF INDIA

In the sky over Ghandi Bazaar, crows wait in wafts of diesel, jasmine scent rising upward, white *malas* invoking the gods. I'm on a lifetime search for milder curry. Murky frying clouds of onions, dense garlic ghosts pulling at my body, mat the humid thickness that carries me deeper into India.

Jet-speed chilis explode, jumbo-size, the impact on the earth clearing my nostrils of the stink of urine, the musk of wet cowhide rising from the city cement. I have a theory that Indian taste buds are numb after too many lifetimes seared with hot chilis. The nose died shortly afterward, drowning in the swash of urine, magnolias, and burnt mustard seeds. Truck fumes line the lotus petals smoking in the sacred *homa* flames.

I have to accept that neutral odor zones do not exist in India, and there is no political plan to alter the nosedive. Bananas, molting their skins, release the ferment of old age, merging my suppressed repugnance with fresh watermelon, pineapple juice, and coconut milk. They bleed sweet and sour over the Indian pavement.

Metal cars and plastic bags rolling the streets do not smell. Nor does worn pavement, until the black pitch presses wet dung warmly donated by the Brahma cows. They are offerings to the first rays, like ancient *rishis* greeting the morning with *Gayatri* and *Sri Suktam* chants. The dung, drying in cycles of sun and moon, offers its sweet smell of earth to my memory of all that is trying to be holy.

BREAKING THROUGH THE TRADE BARRIER

No streetlights, only rush-hour headlights flash in the black Bangalore night. The rickshaw drivers refuse to take us: it's too far away. A traffic cop swaggers his khaki uniform and braided shoulder harness with official Indian authority. His whistle and sharp flat palm halt an autorickshaw from the racket of horns. A jumble of Kannada words spatters back and forth, backing the driver into submission or jail.

We step into the black and yellow chariot. The driver doesn't speak English. We whip out our pocket flashlight, which seasoned travelers carry in India like American Express and toilet paper. But map reading is not on the Indian curriculum. We refold the street map. Unnamed zigzags mute once more into foreign fog. No wonder shopkeepers looked blank when we asked to buy a map of Bangalore.

We say our best Indian-accented "Ferras Market." The driver stares at us, uncomprehending—a familiar response. But as we move into the night's unknown, this driver exhibits uncommon nervousness, the back of his black head taut, devoid of fluid and comforting Indian deference. His gray shirt tightens around his neck, his head bobbing side to side, like the beak of a sandpiper flitting back and forth over the beach for food. He pulls over, jabbers a short request. Heads nod, side to side. Fingers point "maybe." At least Indian men stop to ask directions.

Ten more minutes stutter into seven more stops, each one empty. We stare out the back seat looking for some familiar landmark, wishing the black night were not so black, and hoping that India could somehow be different, less deadly. Upscale neon signs and jeans flashing in The Gap misplace us in a continental drift. Memories of Harlem wind down a blackened alley scrummed in garbage, replaying *India Times* stories of tourists knifed at the outskirts of a foreign language.

The stutters begin to vibrate, like the spin cycle on a washing machine just before the load ricochets off its sockets. The rickshaw jolts psychotically with each swerving bicycle and iron-lunged bus mounting its attack. Subliminal screeches claw their way up our narrowing windpipes. Twenty, thirty, forty lancers rising out of black holes, swirl swords and maces, and lash in mute screams, "Where in the world are we? What are we doing here? Why aren't we at home?"

Careening out of control in a sweaty nightmare, the rickshaw bolts to a stop. Rickshaw bull's eyes charge us, like lasers burning the black night for picadors to hurl into the pot-holed pavement. Rapid-fire Kannada explodes from rickshaw's tongue, pummeling a white collar standing on the curb.

White collar speaks English, like a swan settling over a bullfight. He listens, directs, and then rebukes the errant bull, like a grandmother reminding a first son of his duty. The curb quiets as we leave in a solemn wake. The driver, neck comfortable inside his shirt, focuses on guiding his foreign guests.

The flurry and fear that crowded up to that moment vanish into the peace of restored innocence vacating a confession booth. An almost royal dignity surrounds the rickshaw. Nothing changes. Nature is simple orderliness. We are human beings. The chauffeur is honored to do his work. No one speaks for twenty minutes.

We arrive at a temple, the meeting point for thirty-five rupees agreed upon one hour before. Eyes exchange, hand to hand, one hundred rupees: a whisper of encouragement from God.

The Hindu Auctioneer

> *Hindu customs include rituals of purification and offerings to God through a variety of ceremonies, such as pujas (offerings to the deity), homas (fire ceremonies), and abishekams (bathing or anointing a sacred image). They include chanting of the Vedic hymns in Sanskrit, a very precise system maintained for centuries by Brahmin priests or pundits. Pujas are performed daily in the home and temple. Homas and other ceremonies are performed only on auspicious days of the Hindu calendar. Every month has auspicious days necessitating specific rituals that can last several hours or days.*

I sit cross-legged on the stone temple floor. Offerings of rice, *ghee*, and honey drone gold timbres through my inner sanity, where my spirit, seeking communion with a higher authority, drifts out of its womb. A warped Woody Allen movie script hovers over my sloppy western upbringing, a demonic battle with a bedtime prayer. My childlike hands curl reverently around a slithering mud-wet toad.

The ochre-robed *pundit*, rolling out Sanskrit chants at the speed of a twister shredding the Iowa plains, suddenly appears as auctioneer. Farmhands, thick and flannel, worn denim veins, rained and swept with wind, sit perfectly still, watching the magic monotone. Bullhorns and electronic megaphones stamp the latest offering into our brains, too many vowels snapping a godly bullwhip into the reverent air. It is impossible for human tongues to speak that many syllables, so fast, and for so long!

I try to attend to the sanctity of the moment, but my mind escapes. I feel like I'm laughing at a funeral. My fugitive giggles settle on the sidelines, where I stare at a *pundit* twirling two reeds together, his silent attentiveness to detail like that of a fly fisherman preparing his tackle. His broad hands wrap each fin-tailed feather with the tenderness he uses to touch the head of his own sleeping child.

Maybe this is why Indians are so natural, so straightforward about their spirituality. They've come to terms with hard floors and godless imaginations whispering through saintly voices. I never had to sit that long to speak to God. Sunday was always fast-food service delivered on a padded pew.

Four hours pass. The cylindrical *Shiva lingam* transfigures into a snowman. The Divine Mother's hands, sainted with flour, milk, and honey, pat their sacred offerings onto its featureless form, creating a lump of snow as head for the stone god. Holy dots of red *kumkum* and yellow turmeric become two eyes and a nose, carved tenderly into the snowman's face.

Divine artists play lightly with hard edges, unmittened fingers nudging their creation just enough after it is formed to topple it into its unseen simplicity. Flour and honey milk flow down the melting *lingam* into a vat. A white-robed priest sprinkles the sanctified liquid over the crowd. It melts like snowflakes on my forehead, cool and beyond recriminations.

In the 7-11 Store of the Gods

I

The complete history of mankind smiles in the holy woman's soft eyes, her thirty-eight years erased in God-realized sainthood. "Why so many gods and goddesses in India? For the convenience of the people. If there are throngs of people heading the same place, better to have many doors."

Simple! Like India, where small shop vendors lay claim to every corner of the cluttered block to hawk dusty cartons of Kellogg's Wheat Flakes and Britannia Milk Bikis. Lottery tickets, suspended as paper ribbons, flutter with plastic strips of Organics shampoo dangling like rows of packaged condoms.

There is always a multi-colorful god framed over the goods, the presiding deity honored with a garland of flowers and a stick of sandalwood or frangipani incense. The not-so-ardent mount the picture anyway, just in case: it's good business. The accountant smiles, eyes clear as his brown skin, "For every Indian, there are four gods."

The *Times of India* lists movies in one column, theater dates in a second, and spiritual discourses by the holy in a third. Like a baseball score, God comes to you, not just on Sunday. And Hindus come to Him or Her, one thousand names for God melded in their tongues like telephone numbers.

"There is only one God, the same God for all, but He/She takes many forms, coming to us according to our need, the way we wear different clothes for different occasions."

In America I thought God was only vast auspicious vagueness, watching me, seeing how well I'm doing plugging up the fissures that leak various grades of slick from my incomplete view of the cosmos. Slow rearrangements enter and exit my brain. I am a bankbook that must be balanced, and God somehow plays the lead in moving the figures.

"It's time to close the account on greed."

II

The sun, a coral bead, warms the Bay of Bengal. Waves, eyelets of peacock feathers on crimson silk, open inside the folds of a woman's hands, resting after another day of grinding chick peas and *chapati* flour. A picture of *Lord Ram* overhead could be alive, the hands of the sleeping woman fall so content.

The bride and groom are orphans, sixteen and eighteen, and never owned new clothes. But they walk fifty miles to have their wedding witnessed by the Divine Mother. She is meditating in the jungle far beyond human communication. She arrives unannounced, unexpected, on time. The saint's mother wraps the unknown bride and groom in the wedding silk she was saving for her own son's marriage.

Doll-size beds and rustic cloth figures suspend from the holy mango tree of Ekambareswarar. They hang like voodoo dolls: the beds, prayers for conception; the dolls, thanks for the child.

III

Humming sounds under the noise of commercial streets in India: sacred chants and holy songs. A vendor bows his head before entering his shop. He bends, touching his hands from his heart to the floor, then back to his heart and indrawn eyes. He turns to the picture of God and repeats the silent ritual, wandering with saints and mendicants, bowls extended for gifts from God. A bell rings. The register opens the 7-11 store where no rupees are exchanged.

HYBRID LOVE AFFAIR

>   *India "incinerates your agenda."*
> —A. Cushman & J. Jones, *From Here to Nirvana*

After-shocks of meeting India: disintegration of my evaluation process. I look at every Indian now with a quiet feeling; we share something intimate, some detail of God as human, previously overlooked in my upbringing. My body is warm from the flame of a burning *ghee* lamp opening in my heart, in an offering to the silent presence holding us divine.

But the after-taste of too much, too many, pommels my reverie. Spicy chili peppers claw acidic talons into my once calm interiors. Diesel-choked air locks my windpipe in an inescapable wheeze and smudges my face with soot like a street waif's make-up. Noisy cities overwhelm with way too many people.

Indians don't seem to mind the racket or the close proximity of another body squeezed into non-existent space. Six inches of bare temple floor between me and another woman is a luxurious invitation for a third woman to wedge her body between us. She rests contentedly, legs crossed, bony kneecaps poked into my knees, her hipbone crowding its meaty war with mine. The press of human bodies eager for divine grace is a given; the smell of garlic is an extra human touch.

To Indians all that is divine eternally tolerates, leaving bureaucratic inefficiency to elevate everyday tasks to macro-demonic battles. Telephones connect and disconnect at will; water faucets, toilets and people never quite do their job; reconfirmed appointments materialize an hour late, or vanish entirely, as though the air is too thin for sound to register on the eardrum and click open the memory bank. A cheerful smile and a shrug about "Indian standard time" is all I get for an apology. Or the forgotten appointment may be beyond recall, and all I hear at the other end of the phone is blank space and a curious, "Tell me."

I greet every western traveler in India in an unspoken bond of mutual hopelessness. We know why we must go to our separate rooms, close the door, lock it firmly, the echo of the metal key clinking through the nine-by-nine feet of empty space, reserved just for one body, alone with a sense of order. We still hear the city, but it is not the primordial roar, only the high-decibel spikes of horns and bus acceleration, only the voices jumbled in close proximity. The door and nine feet somehow secure us inside a buffer from all that is too much, too Indian for our hybrid western-eastern love affair.

Knee-jerk spindles still skirmish in the distant subconscious; 'yes' and 'no' fire back and forth. In a last purge of defensive lines, we either surrender our logical parameters for space, silence, and orderliness, and merge with India's boundless, all-inclusive body, or we change our plane tickets and count the days for our retreat, to what we remember of home, clean and quiet.

But the nine-by-nine buffer seduces me inside a temporary cease-fire. In the quietness I hear whispers and images seeping subtler shades of color into my black and white wardrobe. Soft folds of saris gather in the silk wind. Cool sandalwood scent pours its indiscriminate awakening through my pores. Evening *aarati* flames flicker their offerings of love into gold and brass similes of God. Temple bells ring over the drone of Sanskrit codes, releasing the spiritual cosmos from the void. I feel intermittent waves of realization that underneath the assault to my senses is an opening that silences the too much into not enough. I want more.

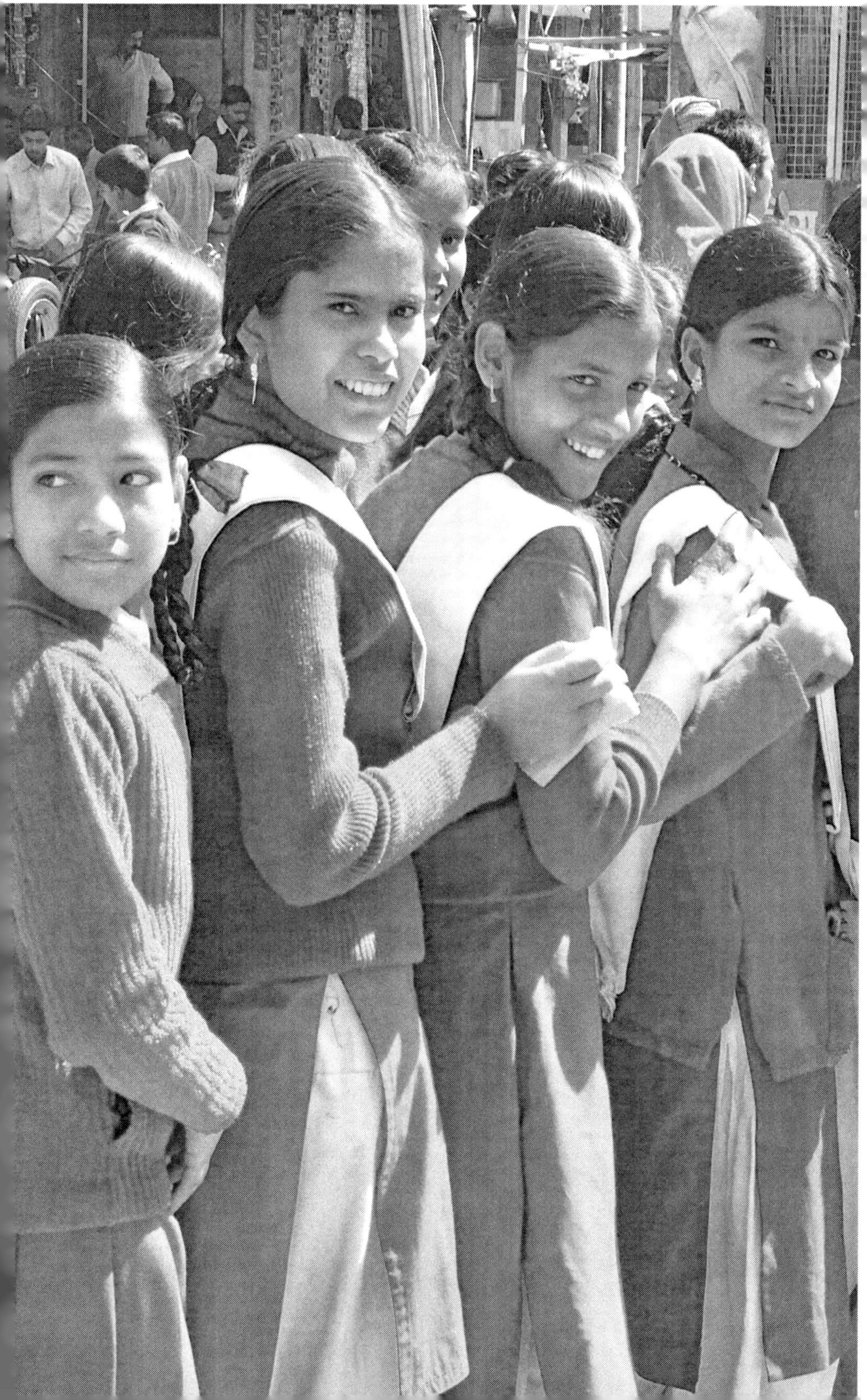

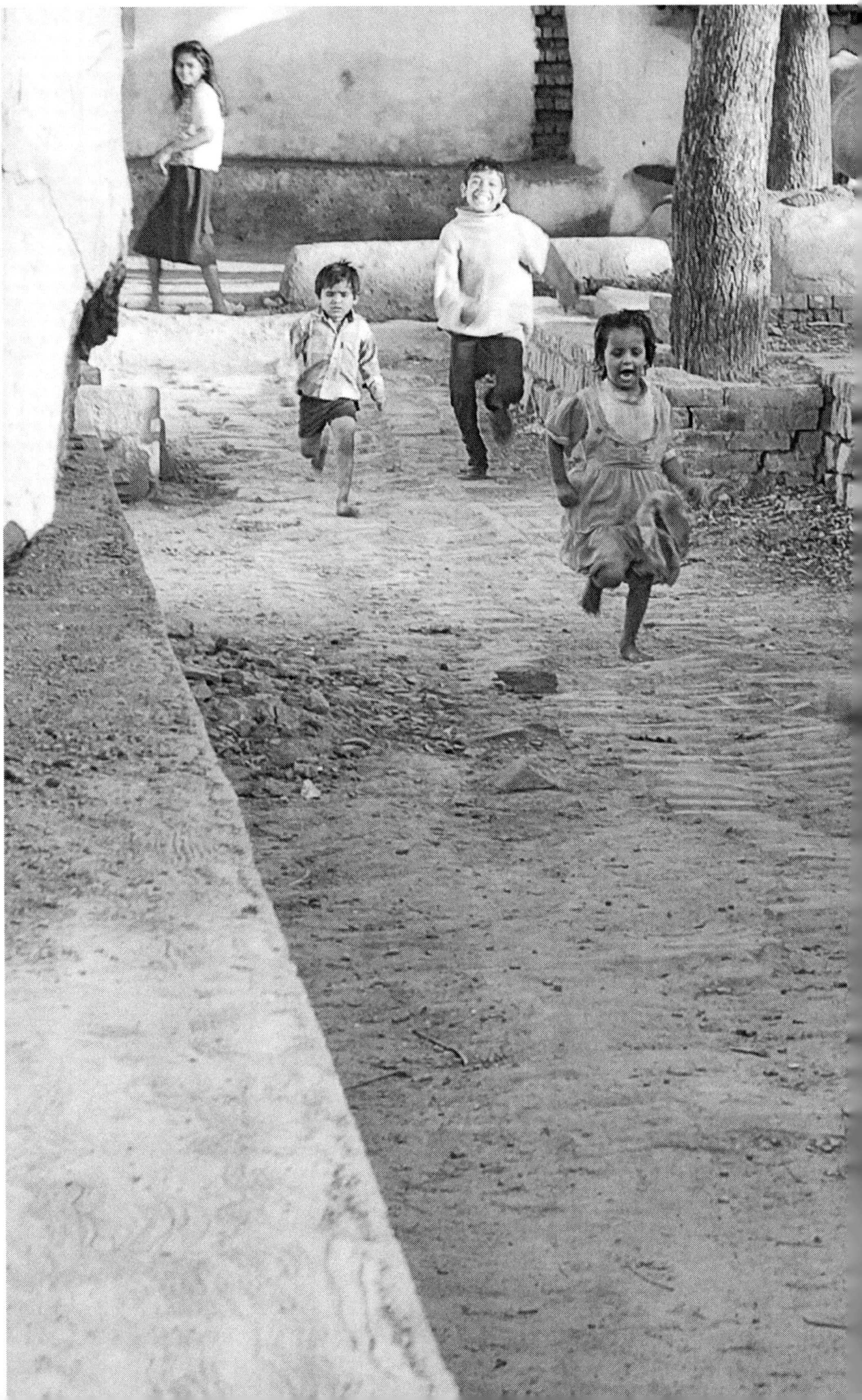

II
"Hello Auntie"

They enter your room without knocking, don't mind if you are wearing pajamas or a holey T-shirt, and always want to know, "How much cost?"

Ahimsa

"Do you sell flyswatters?"

The young salesclerk looks at me blankly.

Presuming it is her limited English and my ignorance of Kannada that is the problem, I slip into a mini-charade game, swinging my arm and flipping my wrist as I gesture to a spot I am trying to hit. She directs me to the badminton rackets. Three salesclerks and one English-speaking manager later, I exit empty-handed, with only the memory of blank faces curious why I would want to kill a fly.

During the ritual *puja*, a tiny mouse scoots across the temple floor between the bent knees of squatting Indians. Women do not shriek and jump up. Men do not rush to play Sir Galahad, unfurling swords against the rude intruder. A few faces glance at the gentle scamp. Hips adjust their weight to accommodate his free path. The mouse blends into the white pant legs and sari folds and is forgotten.

Biting fire ants march along their well-worn trail, unfazed by the human invaders laying mats over the grass to listen to evening *satsang*. A woman whispers to a girl who returns minutes later with turmeric powder. It is sprinkled over the ants' path to ward them away. The discourse continues uninterrupted.

My book on South Indian customs says the colorful Rangouli designs that Indian women craft on the doorstep of their homes with flower petals or chalk originally contained sugar to feed the ants, so they would not have to enter the home looking for food.

A man in a suit and tie stops his car on a busy street on his way to work. He walks over to a cow sitting undisturbed in the middle of traffic. He bends down and touches his hands to the cow, then touches his hands toward his eyes, forehead, and heart in a ritual gesture of devotion. Having received the mother cow's blessing, he returns to his car and proceeds on his way.

Pearls Culture Peacefulness

It is quiet inside gentleness,
the memory of Indians' silent faces,
curious
why I would want to kill a fly.

This is the country where Hindus and Muslims kill each other
over territorial rights to Kashmir;
this, the same country
where *ahimsa*, non-violence, is a tenet,
like one of the ten commandments.

I can feel Mahatma Gandhi,
his country sitting in non-combative silence
under the beatings: wooden clubs, bullets
crushing blood from flesh.

How far can *ahimsa* penetrate my western-bred mind
before it crosses my border into insanity?
"Thou shalt not kill"
downsized to impracticality?
Foreclosed for lack of funds?

Where is the gentle hand of Christ,
of Saint Francis of Assisi
cupping a baby sparrow with his fingers?

Have we disconnected so far?
Nature reduced to pet cats and dogs,
the rest up for slaughter?

Isn't it natural?
Doesn't everyone kill
flies?

Cross-Cultural Lightning

Lightning is rare in a sunny sky, morning rays shaving the terra cotta on a row of tourist bungalows still sleeping. We emerge from our neighboring cottages simultaneously, two lone bodies converging in the stone walkway. I had never met you before, but you don't care. You skip your little-boy chubby knees into my path, then shine two black Indian eyes, eye-sockets over-sized the way only a child can smile, heart flung open without any notice of hinges.

Your cherub cheeks burst skyward with the explosion, blowing me into the tropical air with the playful squawking of parrots. Baby monkeys curl up warm to my skin. Fifty-two years of emotional control shatters. Before I reach earth, you bolt me to the rusty red rooftop in the middle of the subcontinent with a piquant, pint-sized Indian-English, "Hello auntie!"

Four-year-old recessive genes unleash from my body into the once sedate morning. The "click, click" of geckos catches in my blood where northern Ontario crickets burrow with my bones. The Indian air chuckles with me in the blue silence of home.

You do not stop to reconsider your joy, approaching me as though we had hugged before, many times, in the same ancient sun, swirling batons over the earth, catching fragments of light the fireflies left us. They are miniature stars to pocket for display later, spread out over the bed. Our curiosity holds us staring, wondering how seashells form or what makes the sky sound like grandmothers calling our names.

Then you disappear into the day, cycling in my mind like a childhood memory of a Ferris wheel, you spinning up one path, me twirling down the other, amber and crimson carnival lanterns twinkling in heaven.

THE SILK SELL

Sankar is only a boy, but he can sell softer than a whispered prayer. Angels and icicles hang on his quiet black eyes. Slim and still as a moonlit palm, he waits in the crowd of white and brown tourists that mill like candle wax inching down the path of least resistance.

We don't want a fast-pitch street hawker thrusting a fist of magazines through our open taxi window, nor the cling-and-bake burnout of a child hound following us until we donate to the picture of *Lord Ram*. We don't want a salesman at all. But this is India and we know better. As we enter the ruins of seventh century figures carved in Mamallapuram's rocks, *Lord Krishna's* butterball balances like a gigantic stone planet ready to roll down the smooth sloping ledge.

"Which country are you coming?" lilts at us like miniature brass bells, the tinkling skidding to a stop four feet off the ground, heart level. He doesn't stab his hand out in beg mode or even ask to be our guide, but simply slips along beside us, a silent star joining old memories with mom and dad. He listens to our solitary footsteps aged from many bodies, carols singing over the cold snow. South India feels warm and languid. His eyes are still, mind muted like he has been where we were.

"Better this way," cautions his small raised hand, child prince grown to Gilgamesh. His tiny steps chisel ridges into graying histories of jeweled ladies who once bathed in rainwater trapped in a square pool cut deep into the rock. "Men bathed over there." The horizon tilts flat over the round granite.

It becomes quiet on top of the smooth ledge of stone. The once frenzied buzzing and gnatting of vendors and archeological "experts" that followed us vanishes inside an honor code of guardian guides. We are Sankar's, his own Pallava tigers to scoot over the stones, reviving heroics of warrior goddesses and demons descended to earth. Sankar likes going to school. He likes playing wage earner for mother and baby sisters.

Our large western feet squint into undersized ladder steps carved into the granite. Human and divine eyes stare at us. *Sesha* the serpent coils to form a bed under *Lord Vishnu's* sleeping body, his giant legs and arms frozen in their prehistoric birthplace. Goddess *Durga*, head held high by the invincible purity of her smile, mounts a unicorned lion to vanquish the demonic *asuras* battling in our minds.

We journey deep into the stone. We do not shake hands after the exchange of rupees. Sankar doesn't run to the next tourists; he stands beside us quietly, the last carved stone, a temple cave in shadows holding memories of God in a still-life *lingam*. He watches us offer our bare foreheads to the earth, then motions to the red *kumkum* powder. We rub it where our third eye will some day open. His thin arms suspend, waiting with us, wanting to part without seams or scars.

We sense a light lifting of our bodies where comets are born, then gently and swiftly slide into the unseen sky.

Bull

It is my usual morning death-defying trip across four lanes of reckless buses and rickshaws that stop for no one except the cows. They graze the city streets, mellowed and moonstruck, munching on trash laid in haphazard grief under hundred-year-old boughs that form a tunnel of welcome shade.

I step up to the Krishna bakery counter, stainless breakfast bucket in hand, and spot the new arrival. Still slick from the womb, the skinny calf lies on the stone sidewalk beside mother. Big, shiny eyes and knobble knees wobble trying to stand up. Mother sits unmoved.

I remember the old gentleman last week, osteoporotic back hunched over his cane as he feeds *prasad* from morning *puja* to the cows tied to the aging tree trunk. He pats their heads so gently, then shuffles off, the echo of his tenderness slipping over the busy street as silent little gifts from God.

A plump twelve-year-old boy beside me stands mute, watching my excitement. I smile, "Was it born last night?" The teenage girl behind the counter answers, textbook-straight, "No, three days ago," then volunteers, in order to set my enthusiasm on the proper platform of tradition, "It's a bull."

I don't quite get the Indian meaning, so she adds to her sober tone, "They don't want it. It can't give milk. They will leave it out in the streets." Catching my startled shock in the somber adult corner of her still-child eyes, "Someone will look after it."

The chubby boy stands motionless. "Bull's are no use. They don't give milk."

The city morning stops as the three of us struggle with our vanishing youth. "They may take it to the country and give it to a farm," the girl's dark eyes pause, first at me, then the boy. We look at the baby bull making another attempt at standing. No one moves.

In the quiet death of my mind comes an image of India, traffic-jammed trucks and buses, motorcycles scooting between bumpers and rickshaws. Then, slowly trundling through backfires and metal exhaust, a wooden cart is drawn by a massive muscled bull, horns decorated with orange paint, a gold bauble. Red tassels swing side-to-side lumbering rhythmically with the weight of the load. "When he grows up he will be one of those bulls that haul the carts to market, right?"

The boy grins for the first time in three days. I turn to the counter. The girl takes my stainless bucket and methodically pours the milk until the noise of the city swallows us.

GOLFING IN VEDALAND

Bangalore Golf Club, the hand-me-down from the Royal Brits,
stuffed highboys vacated,
leaving only the charred snuff of colonial ghosts
hunting the portico for rebirth.
Coconut palms and palmetto shards,
scattered scuff marks in the mahogany server,
bamboo chairs creaking with our weight,
unlikely bodies for revival of the Royal and Ancient.

But India had castes long before the Empire.
My caddy walks barefoot, calls me Madam.
He bends down to tee up the yellow Top-Flite.

In America I play a more elite brand of ball
but I have to lug my clubs myself.
The rental clubs shed their ego long before I do:
no distinguishing name, only a plastic bag
shredding seams for an open view of the empty pockets.

My caddy has four children and a four handicap.
He raises his hand, "Wait, Madam."
The first fairway is also the eighteenth,
opposite directions shared, like India and America.
The approaching foursome of men look at me the same way:
women don't belong. They smile politely.

Politics and polite share the same first letters;
so do gold and golf.
It's only in the end that men and women share the same roots.

My caddy does not hold a grudge.
Every successful drive elicits a smile
and, "Good shot, Madam."
No other English words make sense to him.

We walk in silence, focused on the simple pace.
Perfection does not haunt India, even her golf.

It is quiet inside the city, barricaded by fifty-foot high fences,
diesel fumes snarling at our limited view of progress.

The grounds crew of women, jade green saris, barefoot,
squat to hand pluck weeds
indistinguishable from wiry blades of greens.
They bend over dry fairways sweeping short hand brooms
scythe-like into the dead leaves
fallen the same way as a hundred years ago
when the first hundred eyes peered through the wire fences
at me trying to merge with the status of a rental club.

It takes one hour less than in America, including hot lunch.
The waiter is slow.

There is a hollow space at the center of a banyan tree,
the same as a maple in winter.
My caddy smiles at the tip.

Kovalam Beach

Faint smell of garbage fermenting in the hot sun —
my afternoon vigil with the Indian Ocean.

Ancient sea not graying blue
but luminous, fresh papaya
cut open through its heart,

worn shiny from brown hands,
lifetimes of offerings,
lone sandal of the *sadhu*
washed to sea.

Carpet stands and batik restaurants
feed my western skin
caught half-naked

between silent stares
of fully-clothed Indians

and waves of God's names
chanting under the soil,
bending Pidgin English around
cigarettes, billboard gangsters
in cheap flicks

that don't belong,

like one red shoe
in a sea of sandals.

In the Vernacular

Such a curious name for a restaurant, Johncy's! This is India, subcontinent of nine hundred million Ananda and Krishna, not Alfred and Pio or Camera and Mar, the names of the boys and the wooden fishing boats sprawled over the white Goa sands. This India is haunted by Vasco de Gama and white ghosts in German and English bikinis.

Johncy's circular canopy and red tablecloths smile shade at the midday sun, one star brighter than Furtado's Beach House, our thatched motel memory of hippie grunge. Folk strains of Elton John settle us into Johncy's wicker chairs.

Wise ways of nature always move slowly, quietly under the scene. The waiter says there is no restroom. I don't wonder where the staff washes their hands.

Indian masalas and Chinese chop suey are equally saucy, uncommon spices nestled in mounds of soupy browns and grays destined to camouflage a fermenting vegetable. My inner voice warns, *No*. But foreign travel is a constant war between the safely common and the unknown unseen. I swallow inner caution, five mouthfuls drowning the known in Manchurian delight, until one baby corncob isolates on my tongue. Immediate recognition, bolts of Einsteinian "Ah, ha's," spit out onto the plate, politely.

The wise ways of nature initiate their silent journey, churning in hidden passages of my curious foreigner's body, until the black of two a.m. In an Indian version of a western loo, wisdom reveals to me, vivid against the white roll of T.P., the real meaning of the word Johncy's.

WOMEN DON'T WEAR BATHING SUITS IN INDIA

It is a rare sight in India, a social taboo. The women hesitate, shying their new freedom toward the ocean's edge, to offer ancient silk its first taste of swimming.

They are draped, neck to ankles, in deep reds and gold, midnight blues, the black of otherworldly shadows cloaking their *Kama Sutra* breasts under saris and *punjabis*. In pairs or threes, mother holds daughter's hand tightly. Wet feet scurry back to dry sand as waves run into whispers, then crash boldly. Giggles escape into thrills for the tentative air.

Maybe they are immigrants to America returning home bolder to adventure, or college graduates used to initiating a conversation. I first tried bathing fully clothed in the Bay of Bengal and liked it, after the first baptism suctioned the silk onto my skin, and caked the edges of my nude body under layers of wet cloth, clinging, my nipples sticking through the folds. It was cool, lying in the hot sun under the shade of salt-water-sogged clothes.

The men watched, the fantasy of a 1940's farm boy seeing a TV for the first time. Except for the Kovalam boys, who had seen the modern blonde-bomb flicks burning red lipstick on the sides of their mouths, Marlboros biking in from America. They lined the beach staring at the western women clad in bikinis.

It's a religious ritual to bathe at a holy site in India, men in loincloth, women in saris, no one watching anyone, only God. But the women aren't swimming then. They're touching the last fragrance of lotus at the toes of Mother, before their bodies fall into the velvet light that holds us all genderless.

I am the only woman swimming at the Chennai pool with one hundred and twenty brown-skinned boys and men. I wear a yellow T-shirt over my Speedo suit, wrap a towel to cover my hips and thighs. But everyone knows I am a woman, especially me.

Lamani Woman, Carried on the Wind

One arm rebalancing the red cloth bundle on her head,
she pauses, turns,
and heads straight for me.
She is a moving mountain
of multicolored neon on crimson and silver,
no ordinary beach vendor
hustling western tourists on the Arabian Sea.

Antique nose ring dangles brilliant
ornate gold
empowering thin brown lips.
Burnished beads on silver beads mound
tradition neck to navel.
Bracelets jingling on ankles and wrists
beat a primal rhythm
echoing the remnants
of pirate coins and fuchsia bandana
that crown her gypsy blood
red robe, green bold,
black gold eyes,
hidden nuggets of chocolate buried
in mocha skin.

She plops down her scarlet stash of wares
and squats beside me. Only one
bare foot of beach sand
separates us.
It is hot
and the breeze from the sea carries
the musty smell
of sweat-dried clothes,
earth heavy
for such a tiny woman
in such a sweet wind.

Where Silence Meets

Mediterranean wine, olive oil
joining us navel to navel, skin
and bare toes smooth on the pebble beach.
Greek island, lips dripping
watermelon in an outdoor café.

He smelled like India
after the dry season. Monsoons
come so strong, they wet even your bones.
You hear your tears breaking
out of the unknown sonnets of your body.

You realize why you were raised separately
for so long. Men talk among men like brothers
guarding the same thick blood.
Women keep their secrets
only with each other.
They smile like they know the rupture
of skin that keeps us apart.

Indians like bold colors on their women,
crimson glowing with gold brocade,
fashionable statements of godly richness.

The Hindu groom repeats a mantra
before the first penetration. It is a sacrament.
Marriage unites him with divine *shakti* energy
to complete his journey.
The first son promises his soul immortality.

I return from the silence of prayer
and hear my skin,
brown from Arabia and India,
used to heat, used to the melting of skin,
used to the sacred sound of the first mantra
washing monsoons into my India wet womb.

It's a Girl

The classified ad in *India Times* under "Brides Wanted For" reads: he is "fair, extremely handsome, athletic and tall; self-made multimillionaire, world traveler, U.S. citizen; respectable Brahmin family. Girl must be extremely beautiful, well-educated, artistic, affluent. Caste no bar." He is in the "Cosmopolitan" column, next to "Engineers, MBA, Doctors," and "New Green Card."

There is no ad for the teenage bride who burned to death. The older husband wanted out of a careless marriage to a child wife. The in-laws said she was lazy. It was a strange gas explosion in the kitchen.

It was her duty as a bride to go to her husband's home and work in the kitchen for the mother-in-law. She never realized the Hindu goal of enlightenment but she will get another lifetime to try. Maybe she will be born into a holier family. And during the nine days of *Navaratri*, her father and brothers will kneel to touch her child feet, in love and compassion for Divine Mother, Her touch, a spiritual solace for pain.

She will not be born a Mumbai beggar woman who has to carry her baby for extra pleading power insisted on by her vagrant husband. Or the Delhi mother kicked into the streets when her husband learns their newborn is a girl. He doesn't want the dowry looming over his nonexistent bank account.

It is easier to let her beg her own way to Indian woman's heaven: married with children, preferably boys. Or at least to a husband with a sense of duty and a job, like the taxi driver with five married daughters. Some families don't ask for the dowry.

India Times reports a rise in battered women. It is a holy woman who gives them a mattress on the floor, rice and *dahl*, and arms that hug with blankets of "Ma, Ma, Ma" whispered over their fears. Women once married are not welcome back by their families.

The *Times* says the athlete is marriageable age. If her parents find her a husband, she will not go to the Olympics. She says she doesn't mind. It is her duty to rise in the still dark morning for worship and *puja*, to offer her woman-warm aroma like melted *ghee* to the thousand names of Divine Mother oiling the dry, cracked air.

Air Walk

On U.S. Interstate 80, cutting through the Iowa corn and soybeans, the flagman is a woman, construction boots as worn as her sagging eyes. She has hustled drinks and diner tables and enough childbearing pink-slip payoffs to twist her hands into a callused "STOP" that had to be legislated equal before any brake pedal responded.

A Salem menthol dangles from her wry lips, *You've come a long way, baby,* indistinguishable from a Marlboro man. Raspy lungs squeeze her heart under a plaid flannel shirt.

In Mumbai, two hundred smogged potholes away from the Arabian Sea, where tankers dot the sand shore like skunk road-kill thrown into an oil leak, a woman wears a sari draped over a model's erect spine. With head tall, neck long, her arm is raised like an afterthought, steadying a metal pail of forty-pound gravel she carries on her head. Her brown feet are bare, skimming the cluttered construction tarmac in languid lilts. Like a fashion show for celestial beings, her gaze poises far above her body, forgotten to the surrounding clatter of buses and trucks, engines revving blue exhaust through gray granite clouds.

Her forest green silk folds around lifetimes groomed like her shiny black hair, turned and bound into a precision sculpture erected in a temple for prayer. She is a construction worker in the land of least opportunity.

SISTERS OF THE ASHRAM

They emerge from the city noise, two child street daughters silhouetted in the temple doorway, matching soiled dresses the color of burlap, hair uncombed mops of black scraggles. The waifs flap their five-year-old brown feet into the sunlit temple, then plop their short bundles of unwashed bodies smack in the spacious center of the shiny granite floor, unaware they are dirty, unaware they are only children.

The silk saried ladies do not flinch, immersed in chanting the thousand names of Mother Divine. Voices drone in deeper monotones discovered centuries ago, in their previous births, when they first started hunting for God.

The two *yoginis* squat Indian-style and watch, like veteran temple rats. Mantras vibrating through the quiet air merge with their skin. Their eyes transform into golden triangles etched in the *Sri Chakra* altar. Statues of goddesses, three feet tall, their size, stare at them, identical twins painted like carousel horses: polychrome explosions of sunshine and baby blue, silvery gold earrings, ruby tiaras, cherry smiles.

The street daughters smile back and squish closer together. One slings her dirty arm over the other. Their mud moon faces grin a complete constellation of starry eyes charting the night sky. Universes burrow into the holy air, the miniature goddesses motionless.

Then suddenly they pop up, mango ice cream and Popsicle party with God complete. Four child feet pad boldly to the door, pivot sharply, swirling smudged dresses into sparklers spiraling in the sky. Two soot-stained faces laser-beam the altar, eyes lightning black.

Standing in the doorway for a final goodbye, the tiny girls, palms clasped at their chest in prayer mode, bend fully to touch the ground: once, twice, then three times. Flared skirts and child bodies bob up and down like reverent jack-in-the-boxes. They syncopate respectfully, as they are supposed to, as the cosmic authority has properly trained them and everyone else they presume, to honor burlap and silk with the same simple fragrance of confident joy.

SCOOTER

She stands two and a half feet tall, dark eyes peering over the handlebars. Child fingers grip the metal between dad's big hands. Her aqua skirt flares below her matching blouse, secure between dad's bent pant legs. Mom rides sidesaddle in the rear, sari folds flapping bold Technicolor ribbons through the Bangalore traffic.

She is the wizard princess leading the rush-hour glide, weaving in and out of diesel clouds on slippers of silk. Memories of our gray forty-eight Pontiac barely leave Pine Street lane and I am already pleading, "Let's not go home yet, Dad!" Scooter and I can hear the wind inside the jungle of horns, claws of lions' paws stealthy and silent. The forest floor is smooth pavement, whispering secrets hidden just around the corner.

The driver ahead wears a dark suit and tie, like the English neighbor who stayed after Indian Independence Day, his scrabbled shirttails flapping in the air, rejoicing at not having to be British anymore. Scooter's small eyes grab the tail of the driver's once proper shirt, flying around the curving arc of racing bumpers and fleeing tires. Her small frame bends into the scooter's flight.

She will always keep her blouse tucked neat, black hair groomed in a perfect ponytail; always wear a sari or *punjabi* when she is too big to be a girl. But she'll put blue jeans in her backpack, get a degree in computer trekking, and listen to America rapping metal guitars over the melodies flowing through her Indian blood.

Rhythms of Vedic rituals chant her inheritance bequeathing a dowry of five thousand fathers holding her, steering from behind, mother silent passenger warming the seat for her in the rear. Scooter's eyes shine steady high beams ahead. She likes the feel of her hands touching the rails.

The Americanization of *Lila*

Lila likes to play. That's her job, making sure the universe gets what it gives. Indians call her *Lila Shakti*, the play of Mother Divine. If you set out in search of Boardwalk, you sometimes go to jail. It's simple retribution, karmic justice.

But in America, Lila wears red dresses, low cut. The job application doesn't ask her marital status, so she thinks she is free. The Mother of the universe is a Hollywood rap group that swears off drugs just before they turn to guns, then laugh that off as just another game, to be free of teachers and having to take out the trash.

In India trash rolls around the streets; there is no street cleaner. Mother means more than a housecleaner. She breathes calmness and sanity. Celestial strains of the first "Ave Maria" of creation chorus through the breeding lair for thousands of years of Hindu history. Stories of demons and gods hum in the genetic code.

America is accepting applications for jobs in moneymaking, not careers in spiritual atonement. Fast food and faster women, bank accounts full of genetically engineered aspirin, lead the fight for progress. Sweat the air pollution next generation.

Lila's losing her grip on India, and not even the Indians know it. But I'm counting on Lila. I've seen her chant more Sanskrit vowels in one second than any American could tongue-twist a right-wing nut into a pulpit. Even Colonel KFC had to add a vegetarian menu. Slow learners need not apply. Lila is experienced at playing games.

Pink Coral for *Lila*

I wear my T-shirts and khaki pants,
guard my traveler's checks and credits cards,
drink only bottled water,
know I will never be you,
no matter how much meditation I do
or how much I learn about the Vedas.

But I want to know.
When you get the money you so long for,
the paved streets of televisions,
Cuisinarts, Tatas and Toyotas,
the excess clothes,
will you turn the sacred *mangalyam* around your neck
into shiny bits of glass and silver?
Gold decorations to cover
the memory in your heart?

Have you forgotten already?
Western chic, Indian chic,
fast food discos,
burgers, jeans and alcohol
at the expense of the holy festival in your soul?
At the expense of the sound of sapphire beads
humming, warming the vacancy of bones,
lighting the flame in your clear black eyes?
Your great sages laid aside
for a fast chemical meal,
a genetically engineered prescription?

Let's not exchange addresses.
Let's give each other *malas* of pink coral
and meet in the silent corridor
of our finest feelings touching
our noblest thoughts.

Faces in the Suburbs

Under their brown skin, always smooth and clear like an advertisement for face cream, they carry many lifetimes tempered by Sanskrit sounds stirring the breath of god and goddess. Birth, sickness, old age and death, swirl through the atmosphere like lines drawn in air, vanishing as quickly as they appear. The rape of war and poverty, fame and success, are just beams of light and shadow collecting and dispersing over the land. They form into temporary bodies housing the face of the divine. Indians accept, knowing life is God's.

Teemamma, our cleaning lady, is tall for an Indian woman, taller than my five foot five frame. Her eyes open wide, like shiny black ebony, clearing a path between my eyes and hers, the brightness belying her illiteracy. I signal to her to return in two days by raising two fingers and pointing at the calendar. She doesn't know how to count and looks blankly at the neat array of dates arranged Indian-fashion, vertically, on the month of November. When I smile, she smiles back, big eyes unmoved like they always are. The time and days of the week are all I need to learn in Kannada. The rest we know by watching each other.

Teemamma needs only one demonstration to remember what to do. She works without speaking as she dusts and mops the eight hundred square feet of granite floors in the traditional squatting pose. Her arms swing the short feathery broom and then the wet rag over the gray stone in quick arcs back and forth, her squatting body rocking side to side over her bare feet, sari tucked up around her ankles. The swishes of the wet rag are swift and efficient. She leaves the laundry soaking in the large blue and red plastic buckets, then slaps the soapy wet shirts and *punjabis* on the tile floor of the bathroom: loud, forceful whacks that surprise the quiet air with their strength. I soon forget to put away spare change or to lock the closet cupboards, as was necessary with the other cleaning ladies.

The Times of India reports that the average annual income in India is $495.

Every week, the ironing *wala* pulls his wooden-framed cart with the blue tarpaulin top onto our street, and stations it in front of our apartment under the shade of a tree. He stands the whole day and irons clothes for the neighborhood, using his heavy cast-iron iron heated with the coals of burning coconut shells. There is no set date for his arrival every week so he knocks on my door to solicit business. He is quicker than I could ever be, returning my pile of carefully counted twenty-three items in a neat stack in less than two hours. After a few weeks the price escalates, like everything for foreigners. It takes a few more weeks and a layoff before he settles on a fixed rate similar to the Indian rate. Even though it is not the custom for Indian women and men to smile at each other, he is accustomed to my hello and starts to show a faint smile. One month, he doesn't show up. "Probably returned to his village," surmised my Indian neighbor without a second thought, like it was common practice and not anyone's concern.

Given an Indian population of one billion, I figure at least 350 million must earn less than $495 a year. That equals the whole population of the U.S. and Canada living on a dollar a day.

Our absentee landlord is an anesthetist who reluctantly rents to foreigners, only after he is assured we will not cook meat or fish in his Brahmin kitchen. He is polite and smiles eagerly when we tell him we respect Hindu traditions. Like many doctors, he volunteers one day a week at a free hospital in the suburbs, similar to the free medical camps and clinics that dot the country following the teachings of the great saints and religious leaders to serve the poor.

At the corner of the neighboring commercial street of small stores crammed into three-story concrete buildings is a four-foot high shack erected from old boards, like a kid's tree house. It is the shop for a wrinkled and leathered old lady who repairs shoes. She sits cross-legged on the bare floor waiting for business, the red stains on her gaping teeth signs of her addiction to the *pan* wrapped in leaves and sold in the corner stalls. Sometimes, two small children lie with her, asleep on a pile of gravel and sand that was left, months ago, when the road crew didn't cover the drainage ditch with slabs of stone to complete the sidewalk. I step over the ditch and maneuver the pile of sand as I pass by the old lady. She stares blankly through the busyness passing in front of her. She doesn't acknowledge me, but, like all the local shopkeepers I have never met, she knows where my foreign white skin lives. At night, skewered boards of a makeshift door cover the front of her establishment, a padlock carefully bolting the few strips of leather and thread hung over a worn metal shoe anvil.

In the countryside of Nellore District, most people walk because they cannot afford the bus. I envision the whole population of North America walking the country roads to town because two cents for a bus is too expensive.

Uma is one of the modern educated Indian women, an electrical engineer, divorced, with one teenage daughter. She owns her own consulting business but also organizes three charities to help raise the condition of impoverished women.

The boys working at the suburban Indian-style hotel are fourteen and fifteen years old. They work every day, sleep on the floor in the hallway, and visit their families in their villages once a year. They smile and laugh, are curious about everything we own, from the pocket flashlight to the tent rolled up on the floor. They giggle when I prepare to take their picture, then stand perfectly still, without a smile, waiting for the flash.

To be more accurate in my income equivalency calculations, I'd probably have to include every European with the Americans and Canadians in the two-cent country road walkathon.

Ramesh is a young family man, educated in an English-language school, like most middle class businessmen. He knows computers, owns a cell phone and one of the ever-prevalent Indian motorcycles, and is among the rare families that have a car. But he must have the travel agent arrange for him to share a hotel room with someone he does not know, so that he can afford the trip to Europe for a trade show. He says that if he gets to New York on business, he will call us in Iowa. He assumes we can get together, because isn't every American wealthy enough to fly across the country for dinner?

Every time we exit our apartment, the children in our neighborhood interrupt their makeshift cricket game using a tree-limb as a bat. They run up to us in an excited clatter of squeals, "Hi Bo-o-o-b. Hi Su-u-zie." They rag-tag along until we turn the corner and reach their lane, a pot-holed, stone-rubbled street with doorways ajar. Emotionless stares of adult eyes, presumably mothers and fathers, hang out like laundry, watching us limply. Bits of old motorcycle parts crowd one door with the rust and oil of a family enterprise spilling onto the lane. The children recede as we continue along the main street, where new homes with iron gates stand empty of any human faces.

Vincent Ferrer is famous in his native Spain for his lifetime of work helping the poorest of the poor in India. Once a Jesuit priest, he opted for his own non-sectarian mission to transform poverty and suffering in Anantapur into "a humane, compassionate, and just society." His British wife Ann greets me like a VIP, even though I haven't done anything. She listens to my questions about free hospitals with a quiet smile, all the while signing papers and apologizing for being interrupted. Teams of workers enter and exit with bids and updates on various projects. She explains that Vincent is older now, so she does most of the administering to the twelve hundred workers.

We enter Vincent's Spartan office with its almost serene silence. He is very thin, with pure gray hair, and a smile so natural it seems to disappear under the light from his clear eyes. They share their thirty years of experience like grandparents, warming the air for my comfortable ascent to the inevitable human status of living "concern for others." I take a picture of the map on his wall. Four sections of Anantapur District are dotted with fifteen hundred red, blue, green, and yellow markers, one marker for each rural clinic, flour mill, school, conservation program, referral hospital, housing project, and agricultural assistance program that he and Ann have started in their simple life of "work beyond duty."

Aarati lives in the city so her children can get a better education. She visits her husband on weekends at their coffee plantation in the country. I talk about my interest in the spiritual heritage of India, how I am so taken by the little signs of god, like the flower garland offerings from morning *puja* draped over each antiquated step-machine and makeshift Nautilus equipment at the new fitness center in my neighborhood. She listens, but we quickly return to fitness regimes and our golf swings. She is so modern she wears Bermuda shorts golfing. Even I don't dare to do that; it's enough in India just to play golf.

Stolen Shoes

> *"To be enlightened, one has to love unconditionally, even the man who cheats and steals from you."*
> —an Indian Sage

Somewhere in Bangalore my sneakers are walking the streets,
wading the gutters for a glimpse at another lifetime.

I don't know who it was that shook poverty by the shoe laces
and slipped on the well-worn Sassoon runners
I had placed outside the temple in respect for God.

Maybe they thought Sassoon was an American god
like the Krishna Tire Company or Shiva Cosmetics
and it was karmically auspicious to wear an amulet
of a stranger's leathered soles.

Or maybe they were practical
and knew shoes would cover bare toes
better than the fifty-five pairs of open-air thongs
and rubber flip-flops
that lined the wall in an uncommon orderliness,
waiting with my white gladiators
for a richer, more loving hand
to guide them beyond the footprints they left behind.

It must have been a man that took them,
or a woman as a gift for her husband,
because in India my American-size feet are like zoo animals
herded into a cage for unusual observation.

I felt relieved to see them bared,
carrying nothing but my skin between me and the earth.
Maybe I had enough of shoes anyway,
like a pile of dirty shirts on Monday,
and it was time to pass them on
to someone who really needed them.

I hope it wasn't just the weight of old karma I left behind
and some unsuspecting homeless Indian was now burdened
with feet that liked to jog around Waterworks Pond

to loosen age creeping into joints
like an arthritoscope of life.

Maybe he'd be lucky and hear only the swift slick turns
of the shopping cart rolling down Easter's aisles
to the march of my Sassoon Weejins
blessed with Pepperidge Farm macadamias
and Ben & Jerry's vanilla almond fudge
dropped into the cart like an afterthought
that never had to worry about
whether there was a piece of mango
buried in the hill of garbage.

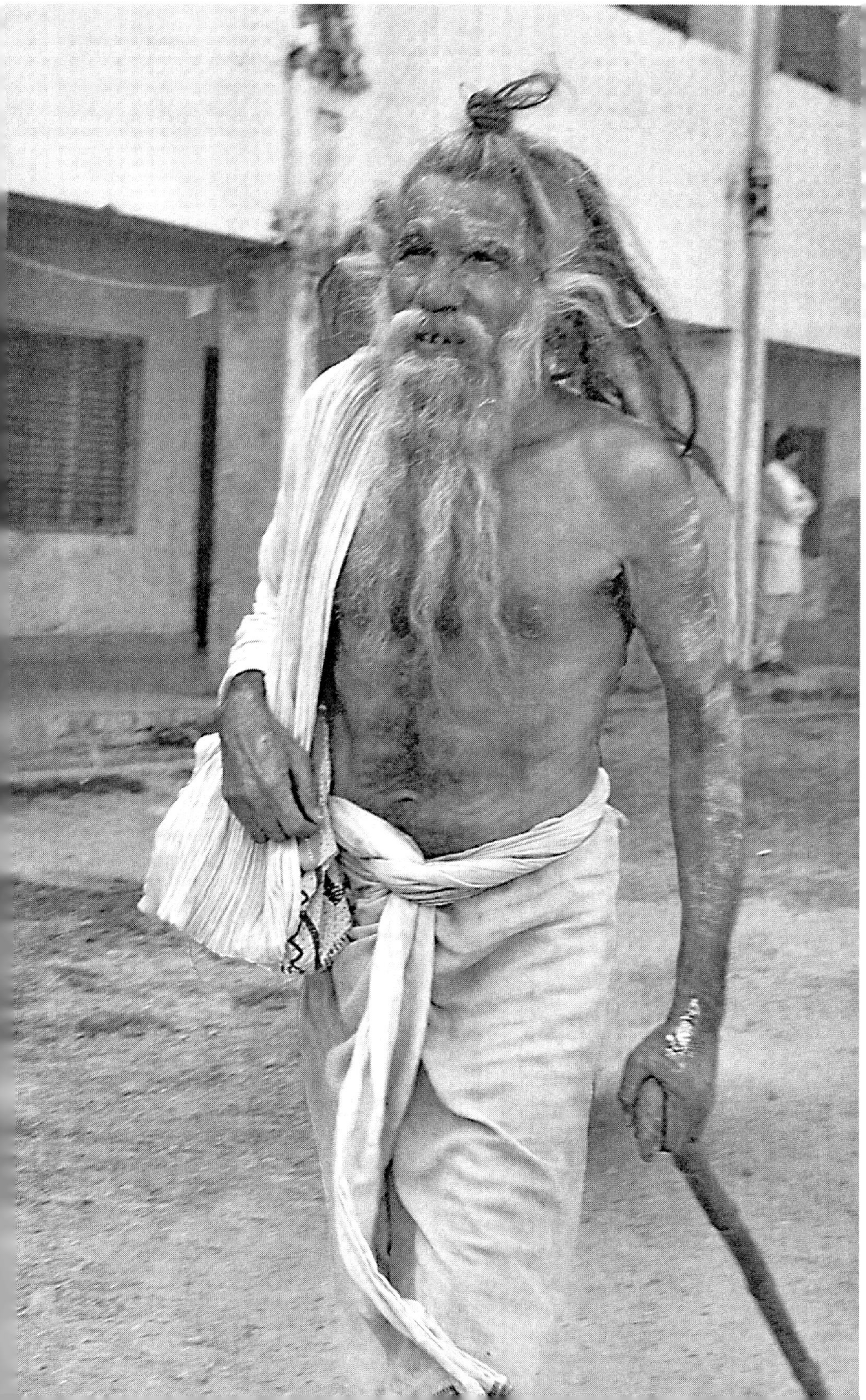

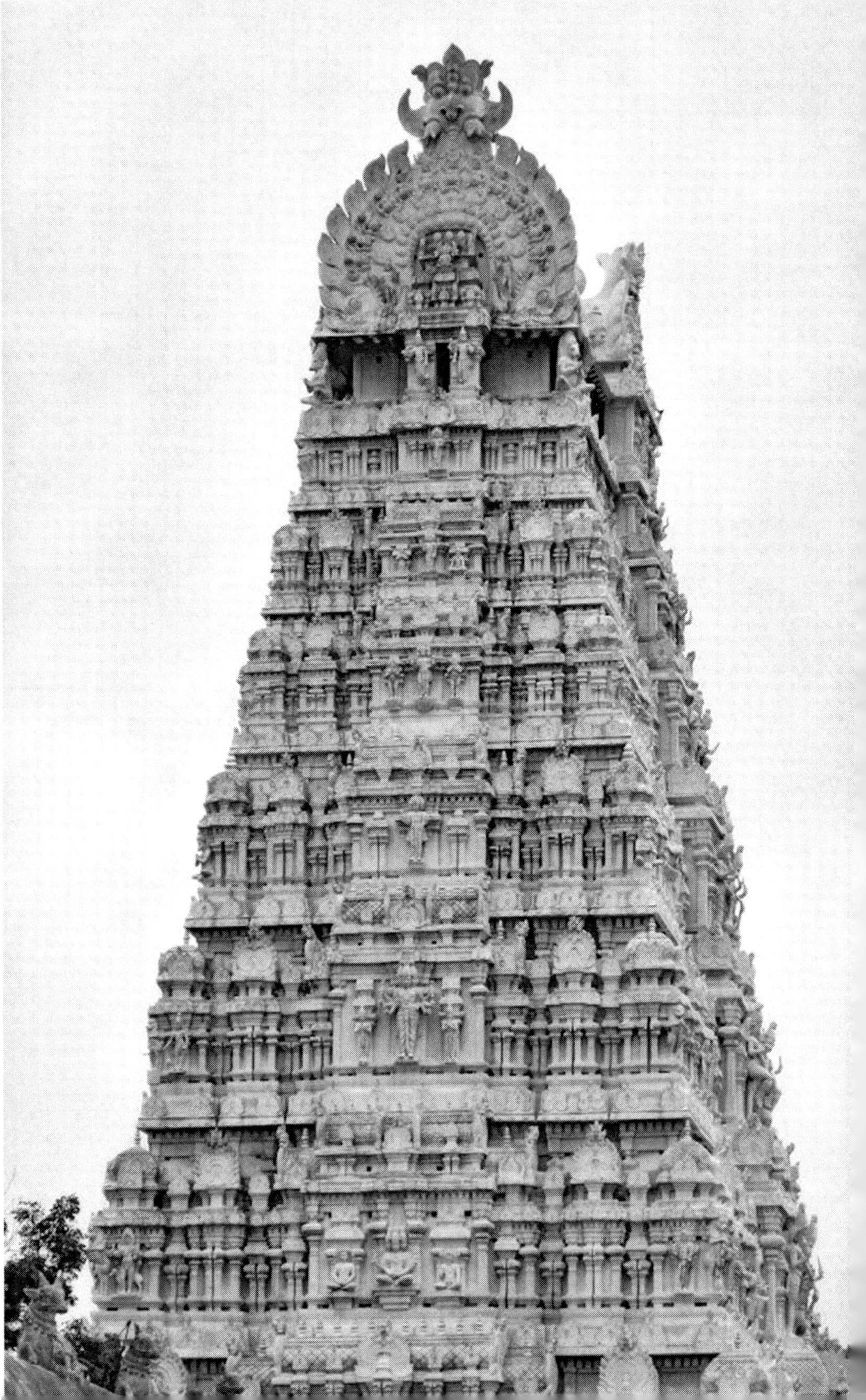

III
Impressions in the Interior

Footsteps of a Pilgrim

You wash your hands and feet,
enter the temple barefoot.

Om, Asato Maa Sad Gamaya;
Tamaso Maa Jyotir Gamaya;
Mrityor Maa Amritam Gamaya

Lead me from the unreal to the real;
from darkness (ignorance) to light (knowledge);
and from death to immortality.

Vedic Prayer for Truth & Light

Parade of the Pilgrims

Overnight, gray streets of suburban Bangalore convert to neon testimonials to the Goddess's triumph over darkness. Technicolor lights hang from tree limbs, string over concrete buildings, sling candy-floss portals into Disney's *Fantasia* and the rainbow-dazzled strip of Las Vegas. My once somber journey, internalized and human-size, now glitters with three-story-high sketches of Goddess *Vijayeswari* sparkling crimson and gold over the black pavement. White teardrops and pinwheels of heavenly hosts short-circuit a smile cycling through my body. India smiles back like a revolving Christmas tree.

The following month, God bursts into fireworks. "Crackers" pop and crackle in a three-day-and-night bombing blitz of miniature dynamite sticks exploding like cars backfiring everywhere. When it is over, the streets are coated in shredded bits of red paper, and the oiled wicks that burned for the Goddess in clay saucers in the doorways lie disintegrated. Daily routines that I wear like a trench coat over my mind dissolve with them.

Then Holi arrives, not in a black robe of piety but in a punk-wild outburst of painted hair and fluorescent faces. Once proper Indians giggle as they splatter fuschia-pink, lime-green, and motorcycle-purple insanity over the gray commonness of pavement and passersby. I laugh, squeaking off-key like an arthritic hip joint under pressure, then scurry my white clothes to the far side of the street. I weave back and forth with the craftiness of the artful dodger scuttling a clean return home, and wonder if I am reflecting a strain of anti-frivolous propriety contracted during my polite Canadian upbringing.

Any cheerless amorphism in my personality evaporates next day in the theatric spectacle of a Hindu wedding party dancing down the street. With five marriage halls in earshot of my apartment, almost daily revelry greets me from a band of silk and brocaded guests prancing in royal procession behind a garlanded groom gilded like a maharaja. Jazzy horns and primal drums herald his symbolic return from a solitary life of seeking truth. The brassy beat of a pep-band rally intertwines with the sultry tremor of horns seducing a cobra.

When this gypsy-caravan chorus locks into my eardrums, I run as eagerly as a Norman Rockwell child to peer over the balcony rail through the palm fronds and rooftops. I crane to get a clear view, to be the bride and groom and all these happy people transforming the everyness of the day into an instant dance with the spirit.

Like *Shiva* dancing for the divine, India flows, untamed. Her special, almost garish, brand of spiritual pomp and ceremony spills into the streets even in the remotest and poorest regions of the country. For the New Year, I watch tribal villagers perform their wish. The men, with painted faces and discordant outfits reminiscent of a drag strip at Halloween, flail and hop crazy-man gestures in the center of a circle of women. The ladies, groomed with traditional saris, step and occasionally misstep, to the beat of sticks they bang on cooking pots. Foreign Telegu chants chorus and squeak from their unpolished voices.

After the banging and jumping and chanting fizzles to a polite pause, one of the villagers explains their homemade choreography. The men's jerky jumps and wild clothes are the evils inside our personalities. The women's harmonies are prayers to the Goddess to circle the evils with harmony and to bless the village with unity. Life is a cycle of light and darkness.

All I feel is stillness, struck by the depth of their view of life. Intellectual critiquing stops, and only my awareness is left, watching truth lay her perfect geometrical silence inside me. I feel this land and people flourishing beyond material hardship and insane injustice. I understand why they celebrate, why they mark the auspicious events of the day and spots on the earth as holy places deserving of pilgrimage. It is not their extreme poverty that is uppermost, but the peaceful balance of light and dark in the spiritual flow of human life. "To Indians, God matters most."

God is not my abstract overseer separate from human life, to be contacted only in a somber prayer in the solitude, but a tangible force deserving of a noisy celebration as much as a silent prayer. Every day is a simple allegory of the spirit, life a parade of pilgrims meant to touch the blessing left by God.

Headwaters of the *Ganga*

I thought you were flat, muddy brown,
dead bodies floating,
stone steps of Varanasi
holding the holy at your door,
their faith their only protection
from your polluted ribbon of parasites.

But you are crystal
Caribbean turquoise,
North Atlantic cold,
twisting and thundering
through buttressed mountains
sliding northern pines into your arms.
Granite one hundred feet high,
gouged cliffs of burnished centurions,
mold the unborn spirits of
Rodin and Michaelangelo.

Spits of white beach sand lie to rest
where you curl inside
the armor of the rocks,
thick, silent caverns
guarding the delicate
etching swirls
of gliding swallows.

You pick up every stray offering
on your journey winding through India:
ochre scarf,
the daily laundry,
the morning bath.
Wooden boats row by
hollow burials
of floating marigolds,
the thousand, thousand
orange petals
of daily prayers.

Brown feet of sinners,

polished hands of the penitent,
wait,
listening
to your murmuring.
Whispered vows hang
their purple shadows on your shore,
bed-rail of the dying,
baptism of the reborn:

God's multicolored hymn
merging flesh
in the Mother of all creation.

Ganga Devi

Birch trees leave their white fingerprints
turning my memory
of what is silent and beautiful,
Northern Ontario lakes naked to their soul,
transparent granite rocks
stilling my mind.
We called you Mother Nature
for lack of a more scientific reference.

But here you are Goddess,
the river running through the heart.
No need to make an excuse
about fishing or hiking
to visit you.
Not a backdrop for a photo shoot
or a sunblock-15 sleep at the beach.

Maybe we too should give you the billing you deserve,
let the songs of the spirit
flood out of our rational mouths
in perfect offerings,
whispers of the night wind
transporting us to the doorstep of the holy,
the honest,
the pure cathedral
of time stopped.

Funny how we North Americans campaign to clean up the trash,
adopt highways, struggle with the boundary
between progress and pollution.
We honor you
in a backhanded sort of way.

Here, Indians throw trash in the streets,
fill the air with diesel fumes,
stack dump heaps on the vacant lots.
But they bow down to you,
offer you chrysanthemum petals and *aarati* flames,
would never think of you as someone to conquer.
It is man that must be tamed.

KUNJA DEVI

> *When Lord Shiva's beloved wife died, He was in such sorrow He carried Her body with Him. Lord Vishnu and the other gods saw this and decided to take Her body and scatter it over India. Kunja Devi temple is the place where the heart of Mother Divine landed.*

Just a simple hill wedged beside the mountain road,
unsuspecting drying shrubs greeting me
with one hundred stone steps, a retaining wall,
and a single chalked graffiti,
Jai Maaki.
My maiden name was Maki. Maybe I am expected.

Too far from home for coincidences
but too old to be naive,
I slip by the sign, up the steps
slowly, into the sky,
where the past stops.

Without even realizing it,
the heart had been thrown away,
too worn to hear its fall, until it landed here
echoing in its own thick amber silence.
I am a solitary temple, a pinnacle for listening
to the mountains fall away.

Pilgrims stand at the edge, motionless cutouts in the sky.
Eyes point over the valley
seeing nothing but Her, inside,
breathing without lungs or hands,
without dreams or promises.

She keeps calling, even as my body kneels
in its first ever Indian gesture of humility.
She doesn't notice the awkward start,
waiting until I am face down, hands in the earth,
to swallow me whole.
I know nothing
except

I am Her child:
lush velvet of peace,
gratitude flowing
through the gentlest essence of me
in the grace of Her radiant humility.

The Goddess Wears Crystal

When I knelt I felt so whole,
so at home to be Her.

But God has always been It,
or male!

How long do ideas cling to us,
grind and smooth our feelings, fit them
into symmetric rainbows
to wear like matching earrings
or a row of silver war medals?
We color-coordinate for a few shiny moments,
then place our conceptual jewelry in a box
of honor and eternal preservation.
The metal remains intact
but the luster vanishes.

We can buy new decorations
or decide to wear nothing.

Crystal beads permit the clear passage
of every color.

MOTHER GOD

I was raised a Lutheran with only a Father, Son, and Holy Ghost.
But I kneel in Indian temples to Mother,
Her thousand names burned into the breath of my woman's body.

SCUPLTOR OF BELUR

> *The Belur temple was constructed over a period of 125 years from the 11th to the 13th centuries. It is one of five remaining Holyasa kingdom temples noted for their beautiful sculptures*

You carved your life into the dancing goddess,
her round breasts and wide hips, lush curves
under downcast eyes
drawn inward.
She was dancing for God.

You breathed her breath
inside the black stone, whispering
a trail of delicate vines, curling
and bending over her head
in intricate communion
with the halo you bestowed on her.

You sheltered her
inside the cylindrical form of *Shiva*:
ebony *lingam* of inner solitude
and formless dispassion
that your warm hands and steel precision
cut into, exposed to the world.

He was dancing as you,
like your father before you
and your son after you,
great-great-grandsons and their sons too.

You did not ask for money or even food,
only the chance to dance with the goddess,
her rhythmic arms and legs arching and swaying,
hands posed in sacred *mudras*
channeling hidden energy,
lifting bare feet and pointed toes
in a secret field of light unearthed from stone.

You moved in the birthplace of silence,
and the temple rose, Vedic sounds vibrating
the hum of her sacred feet.

Muslim moguls invaded,
smashing Hindu temples into the ground.
You buried the goddess to save her,
mounds of sand pushed over Belur's temple walls.
Generations of gods and goddesses hid with her,
dancing under the earth.

Today splinters surround Belur's mystic dance:
broken fingers and missing heads,
warriors without arms,
vacant pedestals
the sculptors reserved for God.

British invaders took *Lakshmi* to the London museum.
Other gods dispatched to dark halls of Washington tourists,
art collectors mumbling about curious religious rituals.

Couldn't they see you were alive?
Couldn't they hear you calling them
to anoint their foreheads with red flame
burning the sacred fire?
Couldn't they feel its sparks
scattering into stars,
bouquets of spring flowers suspended in the sky,
diamond earrings sparkling
on the holy body of Her?

When the sand was removed from Belur's walls,
the dancer stood motionless
in the shadows over our heads.
The music of the sculptor was never found.

ON THE ROAD TO TIRUPATHI

Married to a man with brain buried in a book on the quantum field,
back seat of a white Ambassador taxi
rumbling and groaning along the only paved road
to the most visited pilgrimage site in the world.
Maybe meet God,
hopefully.

I stare for two hours out the open tinted window:
empty fields interrupted by empty railway hut,
cement blocks, a window,
a door left open by the roadside.
Tattered navy blue sign with faded yellow letters,
"Suggestion Cum Complaint Book
Available Here."

The meaning burrows a natural habitat for a fork in my mind,
five feet from the path to God,
two feet from the iron tracks.

A man bends over a muddy river
rinsing his *lungi* loincloth.
Suresh, our Hindu driver, looks straight ahead
watching for potholes, stray bulls.
A herdsman whips his team of Brahma milkers.

Two water jugs, balanced
on stoic-erect women's heads,
file by the roadside:
one red and one blue dot repeating a straight line
over hips and saris swishing
under their measured weight.

An egret cools his feet in the lone puddle of water
not yet consumed by the red sun and redder soil.
Power cables crisscross the landscape,
symmetrical Eiffel Towers strung
through the neem and tamarind trees.

The tattered memory of the railway sign

tugs at the vacancy. I don't bite.
Even car horns honking at each other
can't carry their tinny squawk longer than a second,
swallowed in the forever
of listless fields and palm trees,
no-name hills
tilted to the horizon.

We never seem to stay long in the gaps,
lingering between the points on the map,
hearing the ribs and bark of the tree trunks
whispering our passage.
Maybe we like to complain too much,
or maybe we need to feel like we are doing something,
getting to somewhere.

An old man seated under a shade tree
nods asleep at his roadside vigil,
slouching over his cane.

We pass by.
He does not stir.

I hear the pages of the book turning,
mute in the silence large enough
for a private meeting with God.

The Outing from the Old Ladies' Home

As fields of rural India skim past our rental car window, laying and relaying their rectangular tiles over the vacant floor of my mind, two old ladies stutter into view. They hobble beside the country road, neglected like the pavement, ruts worn into their dark South Indian skin.

One grandmother hunches over with osteoporosis into a permanent view of her bare feet. Their callused heels and small toes are smudged with the red dirt that slopes down beside the narrow spine of blacktop like her two forgotten shoulders. Her companion, with the help of stronger bones and better eyesight, holds her hand as a gentle reminder of their friendship and the conviction of where they are heading.

They are stragglers in a column of widows and geriatric orphans dragging their sagging bodies straight as the road will take them. Identical saris of rough orange cotton wrinkle with the dust and renunciation of pilgrimage. Testament to their visit to Tirupathi, their heads are shaved bare, brown oblongs and balls that startle me. Like a surreal Dali painting, extraterrestrial heads and misshapen melons move on orange-robed stick figures over the barren landscape. Stubble from new growth casts a graying shadow on the private vow with the unseen power pulling them, taunting me down a solitary corridor converging inspiration with shame.

I sense the rustle of confusion inside me, like a cobra slipping under the cover of quiet blades of tall grass. Where are the luxury buses piling up beside the senior residence to take the old folks for the weekly shopping spree to the city mall? Or on an outing to the botanical gardens, the art gallery, the Double Whammy Lucky Day Casino? Old ladies are supposed to be having their hair coifed at the residence beauty parlor. They're supposed to be playing bridge or Yahtzee, watching *Cocoon* in the video room, sipping decaf over dietetic Danish to the tunes of Guy Lombardo and Glenn Miller.

I feel the slither of slick skin of my serpent's underbelly scraping backwards over the ragged edges of earth. In the silence of a mirror, I stare. These ladies, my age and older, have made the choice to walk miles, barefoot, with or without pacemakers and daily prescriptions, to a temple *ashram*. They slept on the floor in the ladies' dorm, six or eight of them in a nine-by-fifteen-foot room. In an upscale *ashram*, they were given wooden beds. Waking in the pre-dawn darkness, they waited in line for outdoor toilets and showers, observing the holy ritual to bathe before visiting the temple. They did not eat until after they glimpsed the divine face of God and Goddess and carved their silent souls into the aura of the temple.

Now, heads shaved, handful-of-rice eaten, they walk back home, past my white Ambassador taxi and jumbled baggage of investment strategies, insurance plans, internet addresses, and esoteric enlightened complexity, resignation sustained in their simple faces and unquestioning footsteps.

Tirupathi Tirumala Temple

It was not simply a stone temple standing alone on a dry south Indian hilltop above Tirupathi, but an urban conglomeration. Cement rooftops and black pitch roads speckled with vendors' stalls and thousands of moving bodies harbored in the crook of seven holy hills, all blessed by the presiding power of the ebony-faced *Venkateshwara*. His eyes were covered because no mortal was able to withstand the might of His garlanded, gold-draped essence.

In the purest form of pilgrimage, we would walk, bare foot, miles up the winding road, to shed our human impurities in sweat, our austerities sustained by our devotion to see Him. Instead, we ride a bus and watch shrubs and trees recede into mats of spiny fronds and leaves flickering in sunlight and shadows at each bend in the road. An Indian lady next to me teaches me a name for *Lord Vishnu*. I repeat it silently one thousand and eight times to prepare myself.

We skirt the city for a hilltop view of the temple. A tiny gazebo shelters a footprint cast in stone. It is *Lord Narayana's* first step on earth down from His heavenly birthplace. We close our eyes in meditation, only the sound of the wind unwinding. I am with Her, many, many years ago, before this time or this body. Stillness settles through the earth. A presence, the sense of someone arriving before I see them, steps into the silence: not an ordinary person with a hint of fear rustling my awareness, but a great being. Dense peace permeates the earth, my bones, and my flesh.

Every layer of solitary me expands into a cosmic collection plate of being, the passage through time complete, my journey at once beginning, ending, in the middle, not yet begun, and suspended in review within the presence of such continuous, ever-conscious support. The lap of Mother, the same firm hand of Father, holds me.

We inch back to earth and the heat of mid-day via a school of head-shaven *pundit* boys in training. Each age group demonstrates their skill in chanting the Sanskrit vowels and consonants that first vibrated out of the ether to form earth. The changes in their voices are in direct relation to man's descent to earth. Delicate high notes float from the smaller boys' mouths like playful bubbles rising from wooden flutes. They crack on snapping strings of adolescence, exiting finally in adult baritones resonating in unison with tangible images of God.

By the time we reach the temple and the moment of visitation, I am no longer dreams of enlightenment or simple expectation, but a spent spiritual soldier suspended in nothing.

Pilgrims to *Venkateshwara* typically wait in queues outside, snaking back and forth through narrow brass railings. Hours stretch sometimes into days, unless one is VIP or pays ahead, months or years ahead, to bypass the queues. We are lucky and get into an inner waiting room.

When you wait to see God, it is the moment when time unravels all the obstacles that keep you in the same place without your even knowing it. It does not matter if you are tired from traveling, if you are not feeling much sanctity at this moment, or if you think you are the holiest person in the world. God makes you wait, just the right amount of time, for you to let go of your little ego before He comes to you. If you don't let go, you can come again.

I sit in an ever-blanker state of wait, not sure of anything. A temple guard appears to our scrummed band of bus-worn warriors and ushers us into the gates of now. I put one foot in front of the other in a hurry, herded, like every other Indian, through corridors and vacant waiting rooms, to a skinny brass railing pushing me closer and closer to the moment.

One glance for a literal second, or maybe two, is all the pilgrim gets. It is sufficient for a lifetime. I stand ten people away from Him, the line stalled, for a minute, maybe two. Who knows how long it takes to stand still as the center of the universe, to hear the sound of nothing, absolutely nothing. I am aware of the railing and the line of people crowding into the space my body should occupy on a normal day.

In a few seconds, I cannot consume all the details of a massive black-faced *murti* draped in gold and flowers. I look at the hugeness of the image of God foreign to everything I have ever known. *Venkateswara* makes me wait to appreciate what is happening. I must go through the steps in the memory, much later, when the railing and people and herding stops.

I walk blank through a maze of courtyards, a gold dome, and statues of deities that hug the ancient stone walls. Fifty feet past a golden goddess

Lakshmi, I impulsively turn and rush back, to leap like an awkward child, stretching my right hand as high as I can to touch Her gold feet, because Maharishi had touched them when he was here.

I wind past glossy photos and religious paraphernalia, stare numbly at Vedic paintings in a deserted museum, and unconsciously lift to my mouth handfuls of white rice and flat-bread in a sweaty lunchroom of boisterously happy Indians.

I check the postcards and pictures, a videotape of Tirupathi's holy-day parades. Streets of white shoulder-to-shoulder cotton shirts bob with black dots of Indian heads. Up-stretched brown hands, swarming in unison around moving floats, flutter like tentacles to touch the deities embodied with rubies, sapphires, pearls, gold, silver—richer than I imagine the Vatican, richer than the British crown jewels. Pilgrims offer their rupees, their jewelry, their gold, into grand urns like huge mining buckets that haul boiling metal to a spectacular final run of fiery lava spilling down black hills of slag.

But He is none of that scurried matter hugging the power that comes with me, hidden. The coating on a candlewick must melt to be able to see the flame burning in the void. I must wait until I leave the seven hills and return to America, where India fades from the everyday clatter of my senses. A black and white email photo of Him hangs above my computer. Then, in the solitude of meditation, when I surrender to the simplicity I really am, I remember Him, and only Him. He grants me a glimpse, not on the level of the eyes, or the touch, or the sounds of shuffling human bodies, but under the ebony face and covered eyes.

No flesh, no space for me set in time,
no nothing lost or found,
only the lion core of my heart everywhere,
silent as midnight stars,
whispering freedom in the vastness of space,

eternity burning an altar of votive candles
worshipping being.

I am His lap of grace,
suspended sunlight
shimmering in space

held timeless
in crystalline crispness of a spring sky
flooded with golden yellow daffodils
embracing me with joy.

We are one still point of balance:
His vision, my being;
my vision, the mirror of His light
suspending me as a layer of silver white.
Bubbles clustering its surface
dance silently,
a perky, jiggling rise and fall.

My body of God ripples:
liquid honey and honeysuckle, pouring,
tumbling, over and over, in celestial sweetness;
each movement, its own gift, its own delight
in being, pulsing
its own creating.

I remain enraptured in the delicious beauty of knowingness upholding me in the strange paradox of seeing my being unfolding. When my eyes open from meditation, the brilliance of vision gone, I know only the gracious gift given, that He is within me. He is me, His crystal vision receded behind the veil covering the eyes, forever vibrant.

BEGGARS OUTSIDE THE TEMPLE

> *Padmatavi is the goddess in a temple in Tiruchanoor near Tirupathi.*

It happens so fast.

She scoots her crippled legs out of the way of an approaching car by pushing on the ground with her hands. Her shriveled appendages, crossed on top of a wooden board with homemade wheels, trundle her view of life six inches over the leathered dirt path.

Impulsively I run toward her to give her money. Within seconds, other sturdier-legged hands run at me. Anxious brown fingers poke, clutch, grab for the ten rupee notes, laser-quick foxes darting teeth into a mouse. I rip more rupees out of my zipper pouch as my temple bare feet accelerate faster to the bus. The needy run faster, their eyes bolted to the slot machine flooding from my heart, catapulting guarded wealth into Mother *Padmatavi's* brilliance.

We swarm outside Her temple, darting from hiding places in a tragic magic show, players in a hierarchy of beggars giving, grabbing, running for joy. Dollars fall from the once dark clouds releasing their feeding power to our starved hearts. Crowds jab and press into my body so hard, I can hear my bones crumpling under horses' hooves churning to trample me.

But I do not feel panic, only silence: my mind, a clean, motionless window; the view, slow-motion fireflies skittering around a rainstorm. Old women fleeing their worn faces and hung breasts, and men barely alive in their graying stubble, run lightning through their eyes, sparklers in the blue sky threatening a freak tornado.

One impulse bolts within me, the memory of a friend's advice, "Ask God to bless them." Simultaneously, as if this silent wish echoed aloud, the pressure of bodies parts from my skin. A veil widens enough for me to breathe. We cluster into a living organism, shared cells and nuclei swarming and seething around food. Their hands press so hot, their touch a sweaty blanket over my body. But I can feel only peace, silent joy released into the breathing.

Then the metal cage of the bus and the chatter of people partition me. The still-hungry thrust their hands through the bus windows, and urge me for more. I show my empty money pouch and sit still. Sinking stiller, inside the confines of my solitary body, I descend into the cave under the earth, where darkness swallows me staring at a thoughtless moment of joy. I hear only the skeleton remaining. Rupees, dollars, marked coins, used notes hang to rot in the bank vault tied to my heart. I sit in the bus reminded, *One day money runs out, and I become the beggar.*

I continue feeling their hands, sweaty, anxious, grabbing at my arms, tearing into my private world of tidy self-sufficiency. My arms hang dirty and heavy with the clamor of their need. I ask God for help.

Hindus bathe before holy rituals. They wash their feet before entering the temple. I sprinkle a bottle of drinking water over the memory clinging to my arms. I close my eyes to meditate. As if past time does not exist, the stains vanish. My mantra resonates softer and gentler in the rocking motion of the bus. Silence holds still. Like the pensive wisdom of a funeral unearthing the precious beauty of love, emptiness prods. My world of dense matter and careless indifference touches the unquestioning light hiding inside. *Give this. No end to the supply. Raise the world above the pain.*

Weight of the Beads

What kind of a heart do I have that I can leave the destitute outside my tidy "nice" world? Do I forget as a safety mechanism from the pain? Or do I just not care, wrapped in my own world?

I come to India with "Me" separate, like a seed in a void, bones and bruises, the smell of blood and spring honeysuckle divorced from the silence. Twice a day I explore the abstraction. My mantra, a sacred bead, the bone of silence, vibrates like a tuning fork aligned with the cosmic memory reminding me who I really am. When it is time for activity, I store my beads in a box and forget about them.

But India's mantra of poverty rubs against my skin like sacred *japa* beads turning through my fingers. The resonant weight of sweat and heat from the beggars' hands penetrates the silence and pushes against my heart, squeezing meaning out of the words "liberal" and "caring." The paupers and I converge in the calmness of witness. I watch the results of my action of giving money to each outstretched hand, a point of no end to the need, my hollowness, my ultimate return to meditation. I realize material giving has limited power, but the silence, the inseparable me, whole with the silence, is unlimited, constant, total in its capacity to give.

I do not come up with a new scheme to end poverty. But every time a beggar approaches, I am reminded to ask silently for a blessing for this person. In the quiet corner of my self, I feel the stillness stirring, the rigid container of me melting, the dirt and repulsion reminded of its inadequacy by the sublime grandeur of compassion.

Padmatavi gives me open-heart surgery. I relearn the value of meditation, the simple elegance of what Maharishi has been saying, the brilliance of the ancient Vedic *rishis* of India. Keep open the valves to the infinite power of Self. Flood the physical world with spiritual light. Act in *dharma*, the compassionate view, *Bharat's* "welcome to the human race."

Pradakshina

Why a man steps out of the crowd to give us instructions, I am not sure. But it happens like that in India. We get used to it, the invisible force of coincidences organizing our next adventure in spiritual tourism.

"Tonight is the most auspicious time under the full moon. Return to the *Ganesh* statue at six p.m. Start *Pradakshina* walking in silence, repeating the name of God—Jesus, Buddha, *Krishna*—whatever name you call Him. Every forty minutes face the mountain and pray, whatever comes to your mind."

"How will we know which way to go in the dark?"

"Just follow the others."

I imagine *Pradakshina* as a silent, moonlit walk, holy communion with God's sacred mountain in a private, esoteric stillness. The path is paved, lighted and overrun with human bodies, rough guess, one hundred thousand Indians. All are trekking Arunachala's mountain of *Lord Shiva*, circled for hundreds of lifetimes by saints and would-be-saints, feet bare to the holy ground.

Our three pairs of soft western feet trundle eight miles into the unknown fortified with sneakers and Band-Aids, leaving our minds free to listen for signals from God. Brown- and black-on-white eyes flow in synchrony, outward vision attached to the bodies moving ahead, inward vision beading the sacred name. Link by link, *rudraksha* and red coral slip out of awareness, left for the one behind, gold thread stringing a mass garland of moving bones and skin. Men's chests are bare to the rays of the moon.

"They gather the energy of *Chandra* and pass the love on to their wives."

We wind through the darkness, the rustle of our quick passage stirring the still countryside punctured by noisy intrusions of villages with loudspeakers blaring *Ram* and *Shiva*. Spirit names echo through pleas of beggars and squawks of vendors hawking water and audiocassettes of God. Squatting *sadhus* line the road, alms bowls open.

God's name drifts with my breathing, forty-minute intervals, in and out, pacing and praying, swirling my mind in rote offerings and newborn blisters. "What am I doing? Does God really hear this name? What is God's name?" Questions stop in the silence of the black sky, rayed by the moon over Arunachala, a solitary pyramid silhouette for my once dense pores melting.

Pradakshina pours and re-pours me for three hours with only two stops for Band-Aids. And it ends slowly, like a martyr's torture, the ache of my hips and legs carried only by the vision of barefoot Indians. Some carry babies. Some are so old they inch their hunched bodies back to town, back to bus fumes, horns and almost pornographic billboards over their unconcerned simplicity. A metronome of God's name mumbles unconsciously. Reflections burn in the moon, my last prayers for peace imbedding in the silent shadow watching us.

Coral Beads Dropped on the Pavement

It is my first time repeating God's name
over and over.
Like a schoolgirl
singing the refrain of her favorite song?
A romantic poet
swinging in graceful swirls of a lyric poem?
A koan
merging the coarse coating of words with the sublime?
Perhaps, but only when I roll my soul
in a Hindu or a Buddhist name,
some unused fragrance tapping my heart.

My first name for God, Jesus Christ,
burns in my chest like a branding iron.
Jesus Christ,
Jesus Christ
squeezes in the charred residue of rage
damning the emptiness.

I can only cry in my shame.

What kind of a culture do I come from
where the name of God is a swear word?
Where the heart must wear a bulletproof vest
to guard against the name for the highest form of good,
the purest form of love:

delicate coral beads
let drop on the pavement,
like scraps
from the hind end of a dog.

After the Fall (Picking up the Beads)

And I wonder
who this God I believe in
really is:
the one I left behind
in the childlike slumber of my heart,
the intuitive touch of the word
obliterated in the noise
of adolescent boom boxes,
new age packaging,
adults capable of reading Plato
but feeling only a,b,c.

India creeps in like this,
under the words,
stirring the real,
unexpectedly.

Shore Temple

You are the only temple left standing,
the other six swallowed by the sea,
the Bay of Bengal, turquoise.
Warm sun still shines twenty-six hundred years,
holding you to a promise
to hang onto the shore,
earth your mother still calling you to prayer.

She hasn't heard you answer yet,
wondering, like the twentieth century tourists,
where you are going, eroding
into a memory for greatness.
Figurines of man's gods capture stone
for visionaries and blind hands to touch,
as though the cameras strung around our hearts
are not sufficient
to satisfy our need for miracles,
for real air circulating in our dreams.

Silent bodies wander the temple grounds.
Empty lungs and eyes expand and collapse
the crevice in *Vishnu's* chest,
where five rupees are placed
by fingers hoping He is alive;
two stone steps, walked barefoot,
shoes slipped off before the climb;
an empty archive, enclosed shadow
where once was communion
with a breathing god.

Beach sand blows over stone walls,
the still wet bathing ghat,
water reflections for our stares.
Indians in *punjabis,* westerners in jeans,
television memories dried over our once wet skin.

The restaurant has only one item.
We are hungrier than that.

Rameshwaram

> *In Vedic times, King Ram traveled in search of his abducted wife Sita. Before doing battle with her abductors, he stopped on the shores of south India to worship Lord Shiva. With no stones in sight to create a cylindrical lingam to make offerings to Shiva, he sent his half-monkey half-man warrior Hanuman to find one. When Hanuman returned, Ram had created a lingam out of beach sand. The place where he did worship to Shiva is considered one of the holiest places of pilgrimage for Hindus and is called Rameswaram. It has two Shiva linga, one brought by Hanuman, the other made by Ram.*

The temple guard steps into our path, raises one hand, official brown STOP, and points at the sign, "Only Hindus Allowed." The exterior is impregnable massive stone, blocks mounted square to the horizon, pillars frozen into a thousand Druid henge lined in shadows. We walk alone, echoes silenced under our bare white feet, wondering if we are not supposed to be here.

Next day we are allowed in. Who knows why? Outside our door, a yellow gardenia sits on the stoop, no note, just pure petals pouring silk under our skin. Sweet water is always simple. Who knows why I forget its taste or why I suddenly remember I am not alone.

Maybe it is the proper attention to ritual. Our driver, who is young and wise, directs us to the sea first. Morning sun always rises quietly over pilgrims at a holy bath, women drenched in saris, men bare-chested, all hands cupped solitary for water from God. Sacred chants mumble the air. Foreign sounds jumble in strange discordant sanctity of impermanent bodies squatted in circles around impermanent sand *linga* of *Lord Shiva*, waiting to receive their invocations for permanency.

It is the first time I bathe fully clothed, nakedness socialized in silk of yellow mint lilies. I remember the warmth of the sun hitting my head as my eyes close in meditation. The last breath of waves slips away from my wet clothed skin. I forget what I was.

Maybe it is giving up that opens a sudden shift in our command of destiny. Who knows why my husband bolts toward the temple as if on a charge from the cosmos. Or why, instantly, an unsolicited guide informs us he has "our" group tour arranged. He introduces us to a couple from Calcutta who speak perfect English and are delighted to share their pilgrimage with us. We do not walk with the weight of the earth, or even on the earth, but swoop past the brown guard, past the "Only Hindus Allowed" sign and the once-existent life of a previous denial. We enter an age past, a familiar dream tugging at the new world of kings and gods.

Maybe someone knows we carry Ganges water a thousand miles from Haridwar to offer at Rameswaram. Or maybe it is some shift in planetary configuration that sweeps us from sunshine into a gray fortress of hallways, our wet footprints carrying the sea along slippery stones anointed by thousands of holy feet before us.

We cross dungeon-like corridors into open sky cloisters, passageways of sun cutting through skyscrapers of stone lighting up ancient wells of water sunk into the earth. Our guide hauls fresh water in shiny stainless buckets and dumps it over our heads, unceremoniously, in the simple manner of Indian spirituality. Our already wet clothes purify further. Blessings from *Saraswati* and *Durga, Ganga* and *Yamuna*, deities and memories, pour like a history book to God.

Twenty-two times we cross dark into day, shadows startled by light, each transition a new well and a new bucket of water. I start to shiver cold in the dark, warm in the sun. Baptismal overload drowns any resistance into a focused ritual surrender. I am ready for *puja*, an invocation to God.

Options are listed like a menu, priced accordingly. We choose *moksha*, liberation. And we wait, our legs crossed without time, silent corridors in an ancient catacomb. Hundreds of us cluster like tiny *mandalas* circling the Sanskrit notes monotoned from memory by our assigned interpreters to God. They chant automatic drones precisely tuned to the beginning of creation. Giant echoes muffle under Neolithic stone vaulted high into the ether hanging like a shroud over our indistinct bodies. My mind bellows in and out of a prehistoric movie, holy intonations, ritual wombs, Dravidian codes murmuring once again in my ageless bones.

Our Ganges water is not in a silver chalice or in an engraved bronze cup, but in a plastic Bisleri water bottle, its blue cap and advertising label conspicuously conjunct with tradition. Rice, *kumkum* and coconuts arrange around technology. Our *pundit* does not flinch.

We purify mentally, one hour, then are guided to the innermost sanctum through a path of dense silence. The *lingam* to *Shiva* stands alone, twenty feet away, down a narrow opening—black stone, four feet tall, shining. I only remember how quickly time passes and yet everything seems so still. Bare-chested priests pour our offerings over the stone, Bisleri bottle now a sheath holding my heart, warm oil seeping from a quiet place I reserve for donations to a higher cause. Milk and honey, melted *ghee* and marigolds, quick sprinkles of holy water, complete a smile and garland of gold white petals draped around my neck.

The second *lingam* hangs like the scent of roses over a memory, except for the garland of sanctified flowers spontaneously showered over our already garlanded hearts. No one else is twice blessed. I don't know why.

The sun bolts into the night like my lover's eyes. A prayer of thanks runs down my lips into my freshly warmed skin. I touch nothing solid or even moist, only air that repeats the prayer over and over, through doorways and street vendors, cars jostling rickshaws and pedestrians, all perfectly tuned. We glide, one foot in front of the other, outside the temple walls, inside turquoise waves of the sea, listening to everything familiar.

Even our garlands that we hurl from the causeway, in the tradition of a last offering, find the same currents through the wind. We lean over the rail and watch them swirl, first my husband's, slow motion fifty feet down to the bay, then mine, trailing holy chrysanthemums through silent space. My garland touches the water precisely beside his.

We glance at each other and laugh, a free-fall through space, echoing eagles and the rolling green waves, two complete circles bobbing in unison with the sea.

In the Palm of Madurai

Instead of praying in the Meenakshi temple, I have my palm read, hoping for a ten minute carnival show, Zelda the Magician stabbing a collapsible knife into my heart and actually coming up with blood! But Indians take their palms seriously, unlike the nab-the-tourist-for-bucks religious rite in Haridwar, where the card-carrying official shamed me into putting out more for the prayer. After all, it was for my mother! "And how about father? Dead? No matter! This will help him, guaranteed!"

We sit under the only shade tree available in the hundred-degree temple courtyard. Massive walls of multi-colored statues of Hindu gods stack divine incarnations, pyramid-style, high into the dense air. Their ethereal faces, embossed in brilliant yellows, blues, reds, golds, stare down lost ages of pre-human lifetimes, assuring me what I am about to hear must be preordained wisdom.

He is a simple, methodical artisan sculpting his craft in silence, examining first left, then right palm, then back again, jotting down notes like a research scientist detailing an experimental quasar that pops a new handle on time.

I wait and wait. The crowd gathers, small but reverential, leaning their ears into the Indian version of "One Life to Live." Or is it "The Young and the Restless" hoping for a glimpse of romance, or better still, a full-scale trash-out at the wild-west bimbo show? My ego slips further into the silence, hoping for shade.

By the time he speaks, the beggars-in-training have arrived, two girls, ragged and dirty with saucer eyes, waist-high boss lady urging knee-high smile to tug harder at my sleeve. Short-lived smile backs off at my adult "No." But boss-face is seasoned and urges her protégé not to hang up until the lady buys.

I am in the corridor, my life on pause, and test results are about to reveal my hand in cosmic destiny, floating financially free in poetic slap shots and metaphysical holes-in-one. And here is this tattered tug of fortune, yanking my arm, demanding I pay up, or she will hound me until I die. All this because I didn't choose to pray that day!

His words, measuring soft, respectful tones from the professional ethos, assure me I will have two sources of income independent of my husband's. Aside from a minor illness, I will have a peaceful life. Then, like a grandfather silencing a family feud, he shoos the pleading palms away, gently reminding the child we are here to make an honest living.

IV
Beyond the Transitory

Kneel and touch the feet of the holy.

THE SWEETNESS OF LIFE
IS DEVOTION

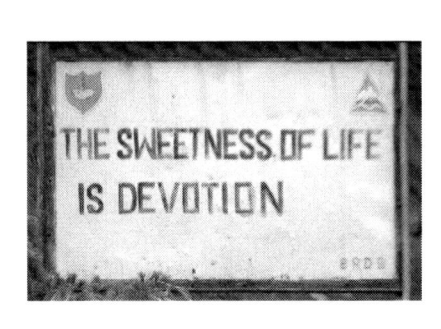

God Wore Sandals

"Do I become enlightened by the grace of God or of the guru?"

Sri Sri Sri Vijayeswari Devi's response: *God, the guru and the Self are one at that level of reality.*

My faith in angels is lost in a choir of traffic jams caroling off key outside a Delhi fleabag hotel, where I lie in my love's arms, laughing at the horns honking "Jingle Bells Looney Tunes." The rest of me is not quite ready to open my pores to the fingerprints smudged on the walls. They smear indistinct memories of brown and white hands of travelers before me, some old and thinking about getting home soon, others too busy talking to hear the carbon stains inching along the cream wood door. It was wiped yesterday but wasn't cleared of the *samskaras* of a thousand lifetimes floating through the diesel smelly air, mating with swirls and hums like a tantric dancer seducing a prayer.

Her spinning songs spiraled into a god before this universe was born. His memory still lives, even after it has died a million deaths: bodies were thrown into the Ganges, as burnt ash or whole flesh wrapped in cloth, depending on how close the third eye came to illumination. Its ethereal stare looks down over my hotel room at the end of the dirt alley cluttered with broken bricks, urine, and squatting leather sandals.

I stare at the end of the bed. Are these feet of mine really the feet of God? Or is this some heresy inflamed by metal spokes of my cyclical ego spinning me in orbit like a golden *mandala* embedded with rubies. Its sapphire rose axis charms my aging eyes with silence so still I mistake it for the center of the universe.

I stand and wait outside the orange flame. I have called for father, but he answers in silence, where once there were memories. Father, did you fade away like a long distance call? Or did I leave you like worn leather shoes on the doorstep, dust from the still air smudged into their tired soles?

My stillborn breath murmurs for mother: her smile, her chubby feet, toes painted red, peeking from under the sari folds, bare where once there were sandals. Bracelets on her ankles tinkle the rhythm of her approaching steps, gold bells stirring the vacant air.

Nakshatra's Ride

> *In eastern Indian astrology, a nakshatra is one of twenty-seven constellations influencing us.*

Nakshatra swirls crystal swords through my night sky mind,
pulling the cobra-twined hair of meditating *Shiva*.
He smiles and twists His trident sideways,
an arrow ready to pierce the eye of the ignorant dragon.

Like a red petal offered to the morning sun,
the hollow gourd of a banyan tree hangs
over white-robed penitents.
Eyes close. Rain drops.
Or is it dew fallen from their prayers?

They offer the water to the morning
and wait for silver showers of the crescent moon.
Black stars do not move
in the early hours of their search.
They call goddess *Bhavani* to their side
but She does not come.
She sends the trident in the hand of *Shiva*
to curdle the purple cord with swift silence.
It is coldest just before dawn.

I awaken in my bed.
She has left me alone with the sound of the wind,
the river water in my mind,
the trident stilled, waiting for me
where my eyes never close.

I look at the vanished stars and say a prayer
for Her to send Him, to try again.

Mataji

> *In the Indian tradition of the great sages, many aspirants to God-realization and truth spend years in solitude, meditating and doing severe penance in the forests and mountain caves of India, especially in the sacred Himalayas.*

You lived for eight years in a mountain cave,
only white bones of snow,
walls of empty sky.
Black bead eyes fixed
between the wail of Himalayan wind
brushing your skin fourteen thousand feet
and the echo of fifty billion galaxies.
Krishna's blue toes:
beads in your heart.

You touched His serene smile
with shiny brown hands,
leaving the earth on offerings
of rice and magenta sky.
The snow: Divine Mother
aching inside your feet.
You sang to *Krishna*
until your aging bones could only whisper.

Villagers carried your wasting body to the valley below:
snow, left for dirt
and bare cement walls;
one hemp clothesline
sagging in the shadows;
empty space for no furniture,
except for a wooden bed
and a picture of *Krishna*.

He painted your eyes into crystal stars,
sixty-six light-years piercing the dark,
votive candles offered
to our curious stares. We watch you
demonstrate electric lights
with the enthusiasm of a bride,

seat us cross-legged around stainless platters
that still wear their advertising stickers.
You cook us rice and *dahl*, urge we sleep overnight,
bundle our middle-aged condominium minds
inside the aura of your mountain cave.

We listen for snow,
begging the full fourteen-thousand-foot view of God.
You only smile and offer us more food.

We hear the wind high above the mountains,
the story of two lone trekkers
appearing to you over the barren peaks.
You run to hurl your body in the snow,
prostrate at their feet,
thanking God for sending someone
for you to serve.

For the Love of Mother

Diane slipped the note and money into my hesitating hand. "Buy pink roses in India to offer Mother Divine. My mother's name is Irene."

Maybe Irene looked like her daughter, not as delicate, but the same dark hair and intuitive eyes of a past lifetime looking through spaces in the hospital bed-rail.

I remembered my own mother's white hospital gown, body so frail, slouched under an unseen weight, her heart almost given up to air. She grabbed my hand, "Ask for something to take away the pain."

It was a mission of honor, the auto rickshaw waiting patiently across six lanes of rush-hour diesel fumes, St. Mark's Crossing. Roses, pink, yellow, red, and assorted unknown Asian blooms fed into the footpath between the vendors' stalls. "These are freshest, Madam." Indian eyes can hear even when you haven't said anything. Bouquets in wicker baskets are wrapped in clear cellophane Bangalorians pride as much as twenty pink-petaled roses.

Offerings to Mother are carried on a tradition of upward spiraling gentle voices and gentler hands, bending with knees and eyes closer and closer to the ground, where the feet of Mother are touched holy. Raju was slight, sixty, with the vibrant skin of a boy. He traveled an hour every day to volunteer as messenger to the divine, roses and note carried carefully into Her private room.

She had just returned from the hospital bed where Her mother lay in a coma. She was a good daughter who ordered special recitations of healing mantras intoned five thousand years ago by holy sages. But She was a working Mother: two thousand devotees gathered outside the hospital hoping for Her blessing. A Mother can never deny.

She sat cross-legged for days before a stone *lingam*, touched petals to heart and then to stone, back and forth, Vedic chants swirling through the flames. Rice and water, betel leaves and *ghee*, milk poured from Her hands: offerings to gods that She knew personally. The doctor shook his head; no medical explanation why Her mother came out of the coma.

When She left for a country retreat, the pink roses traveled with Her, center stage at Her feet.

"The Hum of Creation Comes from the Slightest Stir of Mother Divine's Feet"

—Sri Sri Sri Vijayeswari Devi *translating a passage from the Vedic literature*

Her sari glides, pink silk brush strokes from Monet's angel slipping out of the ether. Then, her Technicolor smile warns our carefully constructed gray and white categories of their immediate destruction. Black, black eyes pull into the crease of a moonlit cloud where God does not stir.

I stay there suspended, looking out at details: her two eyelids etched so precisely equal that the artist's hand needed a compass to coax true line into human form.

"Mother Divine is trapped in your closed eyelids. Where can She go? She is always with you." Her brows center a bold red dot and horizontal white line, holy rituals painted over the last *chakra* of human thought. "No place else to go."

She smiles, like my mother hugging me my first time home from college, and calls us her "infant babies." Flour-dough scented with cardamom, no crust, only brown olive skin, her fleshy hands fold wise words of her ancient lineage of bare toes warming the granite floor.

Her feet peer from their hideout under pink silk folds, ten chubby children in a row, heads propped on elbows, faces painted a secret stash of mother's red nail polish. Sparkled gold, dotted and dashed, they peek crimson mischief at my bowlegged dreams of God.

Sanatana Dharma

> *Shankara, considered one of the greatest sages of ancient India, walked throughout the subcontinent to teach and revitalize Vedic truths. He established four major seats for maintaining the Vedic teachings in their purity. Each center is headed by a Shankaracharaya, revered as an embodimant of Shankara and the truths of Sanatana Dharma. Pilgrims may visit and receive the darshan or blessing of the Shankaracharya.*

Lessons from the Shankaracharaya:
spirit messages tapping on concrete words
I carry in my duffel bag
all the way from Vedic mainstream Iowa.
And further back, from the Sunday school
of Canadian lakes and virgin pines
that sprouted the seeds for the brownbag lunch
I have been assembling since I first heard myself think.

I pack and unpack the essential messages
into a newer, improved sandwich
that I am destined to eat sometime along the road,
in its most delicious and exotic form—
my own cosmic-lite submarine
flashing enlightened life
in my quantum-conscious genes.

The Shankaracharaya speaks to me
of *Sanatana Dharma*, the righteous path
that gets us where we can finally unpack the bag.
Not 1968 freaked-out-at-Indian-train-crowds pressing
our last remaining rupee skin, sweated passport
and duffel bag hurled into the air,
scattering over the tracks
in a last gesture of control over
what we thought we owned.
But more like ethereal wisps
of an aria ascending from joy
opening in our new galactic brain.

The Shankaracharaya's main man adds five books
to my bag and a special Indian sauce

to bring the sandwich together,
"We are all one family."
The younger Shankaracharaya only smiles,
bare footsteps over the stone,
haunting me still,
eyes closed, hands wanting to pray.

WEARER OF THE BEADS

We listen to the younger Shankaracharya doing evening *puja* to the tradition of Vedic masters. Silence moves the ancient stone walls and dusty floor I sit on. Familiar Sanskrit sounds vibrate the sacred space where they were planted twenty-three years earlier, beads of truth passed on to me in a mining town in northern Ontario when I first learned to meditate. It was on the second floor of a working man's duplex, near the vacant playground where boards for the hockey rink still stood in the sand, waiting for the next cycle of winter: new teams, new coaches, the passage of old skills to the young.

Masters of the Veda maintain the knowledge of the secrets of life, the invisible blueprint handed down from its divine birthplace by men in *dhotis*, owning nothing, wanting nothing. It is a privilege to be given beads. One wears them close to the chest, does not let them fall on the earth. Only the wearer knows the silence they speak. They are not a chain or an adornment but a song in the person's journey, points in time tuned to the timeless. Once accepted, the gift can never be repaid. It must be used, not left standing vacant in the sand.

I guard my beads as precious diamonds, honor their giver, and respect the traditional rites I learned when I became a TM teacher. Now I sit in a foreign land listening to the same words of honor. I feel at home, singing quietly with each syllable of the *puja* warming and expanding my gratitude. But in a distant speck of light floating in my mind, I know that this is not the same context, the same *Guru Dev* of Maharishi that I understand holds the purity of the teaching. A sense of disorientation warps my familiarity, as though I am a child spotting mother outside the home for the first time, alone, conversing with strangers, like any other woman passing in the street.

It is subconscious, the instantaneous awkwardness, my tenderness pulled away from my understanding. In that second of visual separation, the path to truth I encapsulated so confidently in TM and Maharishi as the only pure source of Vedic wisdom is confronted by the variety of approaches and vastness of India's Vedic heritage. I feel my childlike security passing, as if the hand of the master is letting my small fingers go, gently, leaving me in the solitary silence watching the transit. No new rational concept fills my emptiness. I am forced to look inside, to see with my heart.

I accept the disorientation, that this is the way it is. Some coaches know more than others. Some teach better than others. But all honor the same passage of knowledge, the same cycle of life. Not everyone has the same mother, but she is just as beautiful for others as she is for me. The truth of all paths leads to one God.

In the shower of acceptance, a fleeting lushness surrounds me, as if strands of coral, pearl, *rudraksha*, all different lengths, different colors, different shapes, wrap around me in a precious multi-garland bond. And I know, with the unspoken regret of adult wisdom, that the one-color, one-dimensional stain of my beads that all fit so beautifully into one spoken truth, one law that was the only truth, is not the complete truth. I am reminded once again that Veda is not an organization or a physical person like Maharishi. The purity of the beads is in the purity of my heart, not the stain of words. I was speaking to my beads, making them all the same, instead of listening to them hum, feeling them vibrate with my own soul, letting the power of the beads give their universal knowledge: the hand of the teacher slipping out of my hand touching the hand of God.

It all happens so effortlessly, the learning, but it appears so complex. Like India itself, there is so much going on at once to distract the simple focus. As I maneuver the exit, bare-chested *sannyasins* in white *dhotis* drift in and out, crisscrossing daily duties with the intrigue in the inner recesses of the hermitage. Parents with kids slung on their hips cluster in different directions, jostling for divine attention to their personal journey. Footsteps and chattering converge, succumbing to the ever-present din of street traffic. The smell of pungent incense and the sweat of my own skin hold vigil for the inevitable descent of diesel fumes.

But my collage of layered impressions cradles in a sense of fluid grace. It is as if a human blender has liquefied all the noisy edges and parts of my identity. I am merged with the underlying spirit that is the moving mass of India, words and feelings richly diverse, all heading to the same place, humbly.

Christmas Morning with *Baba*

Christ came again at Puttaparti.

"Frosty the Snowman" blares
from a Hindu high school pep band,
big brass maestro
sporting a black tuxedo
over a New York ragman paunch.
Trumpets and saxophones squeak
of brown Indian boys in white
polyester pants
and red velvet Santa Claus hats.

Sequel to the thousand names of God
chanted to the morning stars,
a Vedic offering of Christian prophecies
heralding the halftime show.

"Oh Come All Ye Faithful"
marches through Corinthian pillars,
uplifting the open air convent
turreted like a Muslim mosque,
animated in Technicolor *Ganesh*,
half-elephant, half-man,
and *Hanuman,* the monkey face.

Ceiling border of pink and baby blue
Hindu gods festooned with Christmas trees
and icicle baubles,
triangle flags of red, white, and blue
strung like the opening of a new Amoco.

"Jingle Bells" over a silk ochre robe,
black Afro *avatar*
walking slowly, balancing
silence in a cloud.

Fifteen thousand faces rise
above the white, white
uniforms of believers.

Giver of the Beads

I sit on the granite floor, squished into the crowd, my chin pressed into my kneecaps, my eyeballs peering around fifteen thousand heads, eager for a glimpse. No walls hold these people captive, only their love for *Baba*. Like a religious revival, the boundary between human and divine, physical and metaphysical, leader and follower is crossed over, displaced by a unified identity of reverence. All eyes meld into one eye, one angle of truth Velcroed in an immovable bond.

I watch as if from outside the crowd, see *Baba*, a lone orange-robed figure with a wild mass of Afro black hair, walking in slow motion, on pause, around the open-sided hall. His outstretched palm opens in blessing toward the cramped bodies. And I wonder if this is what we look like when I am with my Transcendental Meditation group, respect turned to reverence in an almost mindless awe of the guru.

It seems weird to be outside the experience, a bit awkward to be divorced from the crowd's love, as if an intruder in an intimate moment between lovers. I hear my rational self looking at my reverent self, trying to explain, to comprehend what I am doing.

Can the passive deference of devotion to a guru escape the blade of human judgment? What intellectual, western-trained mind, fixed in the boundaries of matter butting against matter, argument versus argument, word versus word, comprehends the acquiescence, the totality of surrender experienced with the guru?

Am I capable of such total surrender? Do I even want that? To the degree I have surrendered, am I guilty of being a blind follower?

I sit with my limited comprehension of the answers trying to come up with some cosmic perspective, yet all I know is my heart cherishing the glimpses of complete peace I have experienced with the meditation Maharishi taught me. He never wanted any traditional Indian surrender of a disciple to a guru, but I share the tenderness of the crowd, the feeling of what the master teacher becomes.

I appreciate Maharishi for showing me the means to experience the love inside my own Self beyond selfish limitations, uncluttered by anything, so innocent, unlimited, so divine. In the quietness of that, I know that the real guru is not something or someone separate, but rather that universal love, that knowing that that is me.

I sense my life in a quieter, more compassionate tone, as a journey of awakenings to that innate knowing hidden under my narrow perceptions of who I am. Each instance of awakening has been inseparable from respect. As an adolescent, when my first successful drive blasted off the tee, carving a laser line through the air, exactly as I was taught, every lit-up cell in my body vibrated perfectly in tune with a hidden law. Knowing that luminous state poured so much awe into my being that I listened differently next time the pro instructed me. He was not Carl, the man who came to work every day to run the pro shop, but the knowledge of that unseen law pulsing so perfectly within my being.

With each, more advanced experience of that indefinable being in tune with creation and the creative process, my respect for the teacher evolved. Even though I never played a cello, I could feel the same inner drive of the experienced cellist seeking out the wisdom of the master cellist, the perfection in merging with the reverence within. My experience with TM was simply being, the heart or essence of all of the creative golf shots, all of the master cellists.

It came naturally, the respect tuned to the level of awe. The Vedic guru is like the single bead suspended from the *mala* of sacred *japa* beads, the cross suspended from the rosary. At each repetition of the sacred syllable resonating in the student's body, the student slips his fingers over another bead. When his hand feels the extra suspended bead, the guru bead, he stops. All that is left is vibrant silence, the individual being the beauty of unlimited Self. This is the gift of the guru. This is the guru.

Who could understand that but someone on a spiritual path, like a couple married for thirty years, the seamless silence only experience can comprehend?

I do not surrender my rational mind to the orange-robed monk moving about the room, but I understand in my heart something so natural in the presence of these ardent truth-seekers, something impossible to avoid. There is an occasional blip in my composure as he moves closer, little fearful feelings of individuality resisting the power of his eyes. But he does not infringe, simply blesses all with equanimity. In the tradition of India, I receive His blessing in reverence, surrounded by the soft air of peace settling naturally in myself.

It is said that being in the presence of the holy is a boon for life.

Christmas Night with Divine Mother

We wait in a small temple with a few hundred Indians and three other westerners: intimate, like Mother, seated close enough to see the silence in her eyes, the red and gold painted toes, the Sanskrit letter "Om" carved into the wooden headrest of her chair.

Hindu goddesses coated with hundreds of flowers, deep purple, red, and yellow, mass for *pujas* and evening *aarati*. On the sidelines, one potted fir-like plant, five feet tall, mostly air, bends its spindly branches into the room, like a telephone pole with four scarecrow arms. Air and arms intersperse with twelve assorted baubles and a single gold paper star, lone testament of Christianity interrupting the catechism of Vedic symbols.

It stands unsuspecting witness to the best Christmas sermon I ever heard: Christ seen through the enlightened eyes of the cosmic Mother. Shaking her head with tender admiration and love, she whispers, "Christ, so, so much compassion for the world! Divine *avatars* can take on the pain and suffering of man, dissolve it through their own bodies with only a brief physical illness." Her radiance and gentle words, penetrating new depths, transport us into His loving reality.

> Christ revealed in the same light as Buddha,
> Ramakrishna, the Vedic *rishis*! A single breath
> drawn over the earth from the time of creation,
> filling the vacancy in our collective heart
>
> individualized by the mirage of separation:
> matter and spirit sliced at the umbilical;
> baptized, anointed with a code of words
> exhaled so long ago their meaning is forgotten.

I feel Christ glowing in the room, in my eyes, in the center of my heart. My being is like a candle re-ignited by the flame from her heart. He was her child too, one of her greatest sons.

I can only think this is truth. And wonder, what would I be like if my church had ever talked of Buddha, or Ramakrishna, or the long line of India's great *rishis* with the same respect as Christ? Would I have learned about the Inquisition in high school history? Would my golf club have allowed Jews as members before 1954?

Would the movement I belong to even today expel me for sitting here listening to Mother?

I feel my silence, the simplicity of Maharishi's all-encompassing being, here, in the same room. "It is never wrong to listen to truth."

I hear her peace, the single breath drawing its loving fragrance through my being, affirming what I always want to hear. "Live as one."

And I can only marvel. Who or what is this in me that gives me such confidence to know truth?

Seeing a Miracle?

Western history books avoid miracles and UFOs. I imagine life playing golf with God, His hands gripping my aging fingers lightly on the club. But He doesn't disrupt fantasy with truth, unless I happen to be in India, where God plays in a TV series: *Ramayanas, Mahabharatas, Puranas* play and replay divine intervention.

My brain regroups after a fall from grace, notices seed letters trying to form new words around my heart. Apparently, I am reborn but don't know it. I sit in a temple room in a country orphanage holding a pendant of a saint in my hands. Sweet syrup flows from its plastic, improbable birthplace.

My husband is a scientist; he laughs at the honey pouring and pouring out of no known origin. It runs into his cupped palm, forms a pool and translates no known physical origins into a necessary category for his right brain.

USA Today reports that thirty-four percent of Americans have one question they want answered, "Why am I here?" The sperm and egg chapter does not completely satisfy.

Before my husband laughs, I don't know what I am seeing, like reading a poem I can't hear—lines and triangles, silent waves. I get used to miracles the second time around, but again my husband has to point it out. The lady is a holy woman so my head is bowed. She hands me a silver figurine of *Lakshmi*, pulls it out of the air, five brown fingers extending toward me, first empty then full. I take the gift without a thought.

Only later do I realize what I have seen. Only then, in the cool historical pictures of my brain, do I wonder if every day is a poem I don't see, honey fragrant with rose.

Just to be with Mother

It's her rose-scented silence that hits me, full wrap-around love immersion. Like a gold semi-trailer massed in my driveway, there's no space left for entering or exiting, just being, beaming inward, a honeymoon cruise with Mother, captain of the submarine to the universe.

I am on VIP crew, ushering and being ushered to a submerged coral assembly of virgin tears unheard in the silver privacy of my personality. Arias of sonar sopranos escape too joyful for my dense human casing. God and goddess float in silence erupting out of the memory of my heart.

I belong here but no one ever told me. The lace of the universe is intricate, alabaster combing on the ocean of the sky. Infinity slips through its web, coriander waves mirroring the matrix of my mind.

I slide into its echo, two transparent holograms synchronizing. The lines of latticework vanish, and all we are is space, matching center, traveling together, God and I, to Hyderabad and back.

Learning to Bead the Sounds of Nature

"Ahh," our Vedic sage emphasizes the correct pronunciation.

We mimic back, "Ahh."

"No. Ahh."

The distinction between the two escapes the ears of our array of rock-and-roll bred westerners. But that does not prevent us from pretending another respectful, "Ahh," hoping for some transcendental intervention in the transmission.

"Good."

We smile, totally ignorant. But somewhere in our *chits* of new age meeting old, we feel the sense of something grand: names of God aligning our existence on this planet with the cosmic order of things, the daily arrival of sunshine in our bedroom, waking us to the possibility for everything. We do not remember saying our first baby words, testing the vocal chords. But we know instinctively when it is "right." The sound lines up with some mysterious new nerve in our body, the sense of the hand drawing a perfect circle, a painter placing a dot exactly in the center of a blank canvas, then standing back and viewing the completeness.

It takes time, to repeat the same phrase over and over, to adjust each subtle difference in pronunciation to the voice of the teacher. Patience sounds like patients, and to the novice learning to chant the sacred Vedic verses, the distinction is blurred. At one instance in the process, I feel a stillness and peace akin to holy. At another, I feel like I am a patient, recovering from a cold or a fever. But as my ears and mind refine and align with each passage, I sense the underlying rhythm pulsing simple nature, the sense of being comfortable in my own body, patient with being.

ॐ असतो मा सद् गमय।
तमसो मा ज्योतिर्गमय।
मृत्योर्मा ऽमृतम् गमय ॥

Suburban Monkey

The gray monkey and I sit motionless on separate rooftops,
joined by fifty feet of empty space
hanging over swinging spears of coconut palms,
once natives in a jungle
of dew and dense chlorophyll molecules.

Flesh of green leaves and wetness breathed then,
before the monkey's parents could know
that raising children in traditional forest symmetries
would fracture into fragments,
bamboo stems and juicy mangoes
into concrete walls and corrugated metal.

The monkey and I both eye the few trees left
sanctifying our contemplation.

We climb here each morning,
he, up the four story drainpipe
clinging to the far exterior wall,
and I, up the shadowed interior steps,
methodical increments scaling the sun.

The monkey always strikes me quiet and calm.
Wife and baby never join him here.
This is his moment, to sit high
above the pavement and patterned rows of suburbia.

Sometimes he rises from his graying-fur reflection,
saunters, paws swinging along the narrow ledge of the roof.
Then he perches once again in the solitude,
resting on his haunches. He stares,
the rising sun silhouetting him in its red and orange ball,
his tail dangling over the edge of the roof,
like a hemp noose abandoned by God
when too many emergencies rang off Her cell phone.

I chant Sanskrit names of God, trying to call Her back
over busy signals and interrupted messages
on my answer machine, man-made philosophies
of the intrinsic and indefinable.
My calls form a shadow over the rooftop,

the exact shape of my body,
a phonetic hologram, a brilliant star
burning in the center of my heart.

Its light pours over the rooftop,
spreading the thin air between me and the monkey,
collecting the entire neighborhood
in morning reconstruction.

He knows.
He can wait forever on the edge
of the cement that barricades people
and their new old ideas of tomorrow,
of what they really are,
why they are here.
He doesn't regret.
And he doesn't worry
about how many stories he can fall.

I keep on singing to the goddess in the sun,
through shadows creaking arthritic joints
and shivering fevers of "to do's."

He doesn't mind the traffic noises rousting the quiet morning.
He knows they are there, but doesn't take notice,
people emptying out of their tomorrows,
walking slowly, still under the influence
of midnight dreams.

I finish my prayers and admonished misdemeanors,
stare at him, our flat rooftops, gaps in space.
The palm trees do not move.

He rises on all fours,
leans over the edge of the building
as if readying to leap into the emptiness
three stories to the pavement below.
He pauses, balancing
the stillness he has come from
with the stillness where he is going.
Then gently, soft
as the cotton wisps of fur on his body,
he turns his head sideways and walks on.

Three Meditations: Trinity of Beads

Jog Falls: Red Coral

None of the tourist brochures mentioned her.
She lies hidden in the ether
suspended over the narrow gorge
ruptured into the green mat of jungle treetops.

Four arcing jets of water blast over the rocky gunnel,
then plummet,
sheering the earth 975 feet
into a corridor of vertigo

ripping my body
from its cover of granite
and dense tropical forest;
the once tidy array
of flowerbeds and lawn
that organized the British empire;
the vacancy of the now
shambled Indian-government hotel.

What remains of essential me
rappels instantly into her arms,
free-fall silence wrapping me in lush flesh,
taking me home.

I stay with her, vibrant,
my body forgotten on the cement garden bench.
And I do not want to leave,
ever.

Sri Sailam Temple: Rudraksha

I stay with eternity, rooted under a banyan tree, deep within the umbrella of *Shiva's* formless silence. Gentle arms of the sun set over this body, a weighted capsule of being, so dense, so compelling; the one that hears and knows has no choice, it is unable to move.

The "I" hears the passing of evening worshippers, the padding of bare feet, Bob's whispering, "The temple tour is resuming." But the body stays mute to each intention to move. Only the eyes manage to flutter, peeping through viscous completeness. Then my hand, the ultimate arbiter of grasping reality, hanging like a wet mop, responds with a slow-motion lift above the thigh, as if air seeping into a balloon finally reaches the threshold for weightlessness. Legs, arms and trunk follow, released into the air in a mirage of motion. Bob slips alongside as guardian, his tender attentiveness steering the precious cargo carried by this distant body that is mine.

It steps over worn, granite cobbles. Being does not move, transfixed in something ancient, something so real. The "I" lives before time recorded with eyes and ears, before the first spark lit the awareness. Compacted imprints of unconquerable power hold me planted in the bones of Being.

"I" walk without walking. The timeless presses time, compressing the farthest distant past and now into a mysterious moving stillness, not déjà vu, but every instant living non-sequentially now within the dense atmosphere of some other time. My eyes stare, the moon pauses, vacant channels calmed. A black shadow in the moonlight sifts through a veil; a prehistoric memory of Sri Sailam's stone tower fixes in the darkness glowing like an ancient pyramid. I am here, living before, wondering with the silence. *What does this mean, this unalterable sureness of being, memory?*

The dreamscape of "me," as if captured on the verge of waking, steps through an archway of granite into a room constructed of mirrors. Engulfed by crystalline walls and ceiling offering nothing but reflection, this being is reduced to simple perception staring through eye-sockets, quietly scanning the space for something. The room is vacant, except for a small, wooden swing enthroned in the center, empty. Somewhere in the fathomless silence of awareness, a faint speck of attention curls. Worn stone and shiny glass converge, perplexing. *What is this non-sequence: a temple but no image of God? What am I supposed to see?*

In the wordless void, the body mirrors its own mirage, the unseen self luminous through the perception. The swing waits empty in the center. Being senses an immovable rocking of the swing cradling within my heart. It is the imprint of the goddess *Lalitambika*, her gentle swaying lullaby beading the center of creation, its lyric love the precious rhythm of Being silently carrying this body of mirrors. She is hidden in its center in perfect reflection.

Under the moon's slender arm, mute in the grandeur of human unknowing, I hear the Divine Mother say everything, our destiny, our search, when we will visit Sri Sailam, is marked in our brow.

RAMANA MAHARISHI'S CAVE: RUDRAKSHA AND RED CORAL

As I near his rock sanctuary,
my eyes retreat. Knees surrender
their struggle with gravity.

Once-definitive "me" scents
the caress of the invisible

stillness between breaths,
veils of candlelight
glancing off smooth granite.

Once-human shadows meditate,
embracing the velvet air.

Beauty roots
in the calm
petals of prayer,

my skin lilting silk sonnets
nudging the delicate secret

that was me, vanishing
in its own permeable paragraph.

Sandalwood oil pours
simple, clear
knowing,

cleansing the mind of calluses,
the heart of stains,

the history of being
unconquered.

This is

the only
statement that makes sense.

How could I ever think
God might not exist,
enlightenment a phantom?

Dwellers in the Caves

To the great Vedic Rishis of India

They sit in their stone isolation chambers
scattered through Himalayan mountainsides and South Indian forests,
listening, like probes pulsing into cardiac monitors
experimenting with God.

A ripple in the still wind nudges a door open,
swinging it just enough to let the breeze exhale.
The door pauses, waiting for the passage.
Then it pendulums
like an eagle gliding to its resting place,
the force of the earth released
along a spire of hinges and wooden frames
left by the unseen architect.
The weight ascends into the weightless.

The eyes of the cave dwellers are closed.
Their lungs do not move.
Sounds no longer exist.

Uttar Kashi, Arunachala, Garudachala—
earth and stone silenced into breathless caves.

My eyes close in their presence.
I do not hear them through my ears
because my ears vanish.
I do not see them through my eyes
because my eyes vanish.
I am only an echo of stone humming,
the structure of hinges and doorframes, girders to God
holding everything in balance.

Only the still air of the cave can sense
the stillness in my heart

I place my gift of a baby dove nested in down
into the palm of the *rishi*. He handles it so carefully,
his large fingers curling around the baby feathers,
holding firm, yet leaving space for the delicate fluff.

He lifts the dove to his lips and whispers
fine notes of a father's wisdom,

then releases the child into the void
and watches, his gaze never leaving
her circle and swirl alone with the wind.

Memo to God

You never informed me that I could feel this holy,
that I could ever sense this creamy pouring under my skin,
this so simply secure place I am given
to look through such uncluttered eyes

at the joy of the simple attraction to be
touching the red and sacred lineage of daylight
screaming into my pores.

One more chance granted
to offer this cotton husk of me
into the silent tradition of You.

In the Center of the Beads

It's a gentle secret to feel my own personal star radiating from the center of my being.

No wonder the Vedic literature extols the Divine Mother's virtues; the gods and *rishis* worship Her; Indians bow to touch Her feet and hold Her in their heart as their own birth mother, the power of Her love, the generator for the whole creation.

Reflection from a Hammock by the Bay of Bengal

Sacred and silent,
no other being left to hear,
holds, pounds, pours out the center of my chest.

My heart has no end, no beginning.
A vast hole in my chest
has consumed the entirety of life
and planted it inside this body,

under the thoughts,
inside the succulent and sweet,
the sorrowful sand that scratches
but cannot adjust or change—
you, monitoring progress,
the steady being of my comings and goings.

When I close my eyes, only the stillness echoes
through the body's pains and nervous triangulations,
through the spaces in thoughts—
my thoughts, my body, my sweltering fear and pain
now somehow yours,
mine, ours.

Thank you.
It is the only hymn I feel
smiling in the silence.

Into the Fire

where no one hears
but all the world is listening,

this little child
I have been carrying
sixty years
vanishes.

Guesswork?

Who knows why
everything seems
to arrange itself,
the little details unnoticed?
I would never purchase the garish,
almost cartoonish picture of *Shiva-Shakti*
someone left in our apartment.

It ends up in my suitcase,
the perfect size backing to support my MRI's
for the long journey home.
God as half-male and half-female
merged in one body.
To remind me.

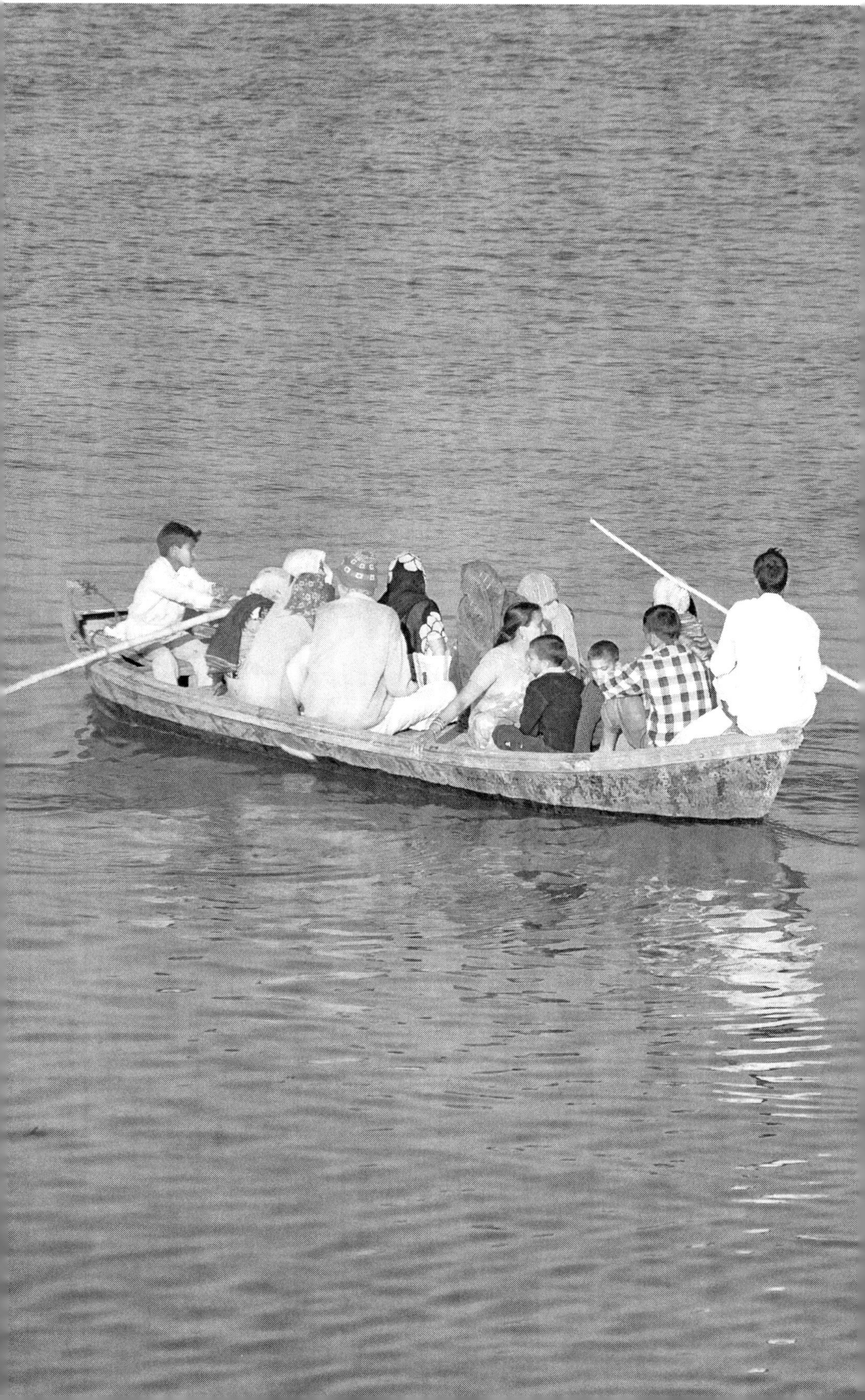

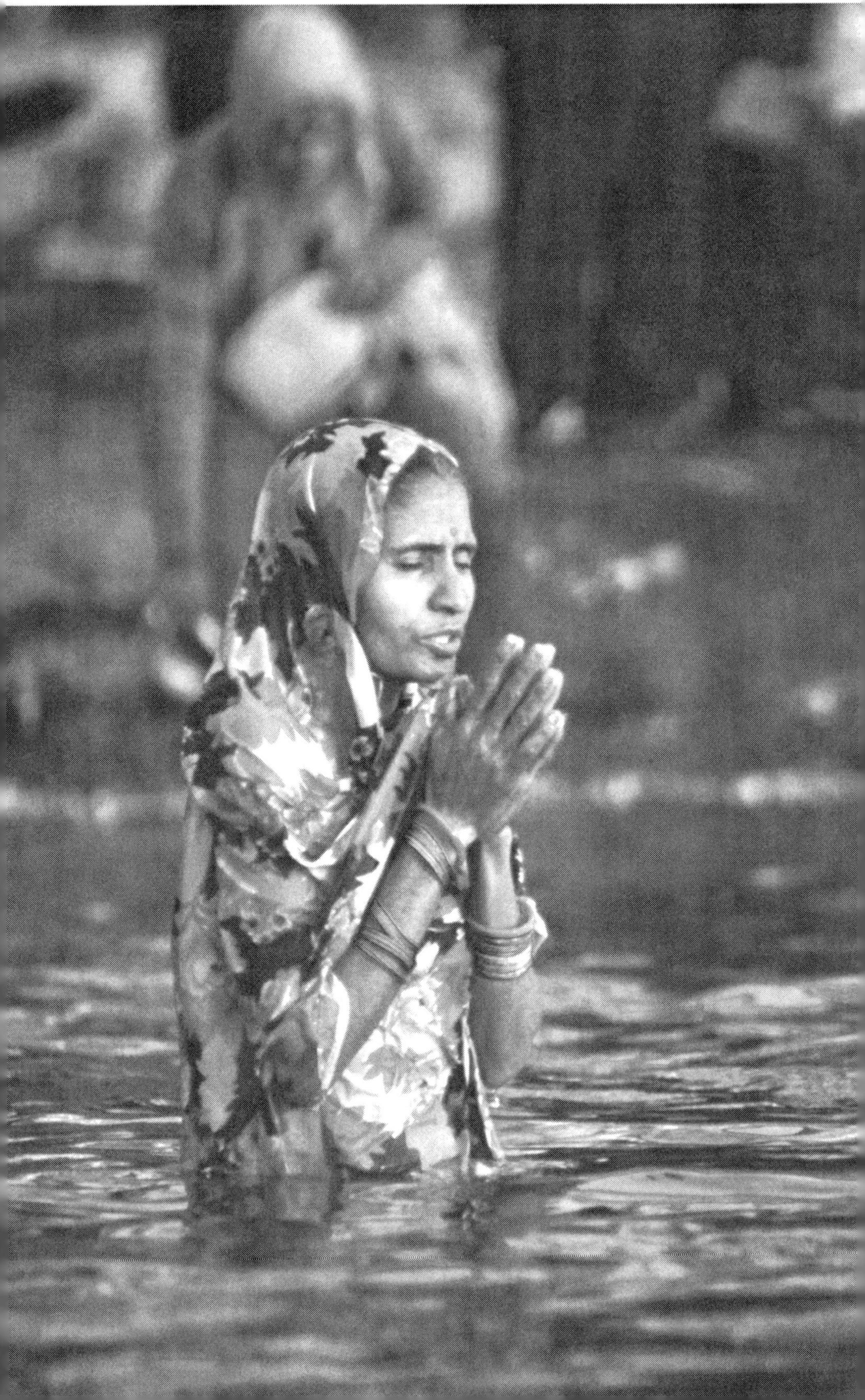

V
Flight Home

Mother India touches everyone,
no matter what their beliefs.

Vasudhaiva kutumbakam

The world is my family.

Ancient Sanskrit saying
fundamental to Indian culture

Meera

To Mother Meera, an Indian saint living in Germany

Her eyes were midnight dark and still, barely aware of the Indian body she carried with her, a reminder that she was now on earth and divinity was mortal.

But I could think only human pictures of her pouring the concrete for her new home. She loved to drive nails into the strong German structure she opened to everyone, like we were her responsibility to help along the crooked trails we tacked behind us.

She touched my forehead without any emotion and looked into my eyes without color or reflections. She was here to give to us, and we to take without any return, two hundred of us sitting silently, three hours, deep in mental conversations with our own lives.

And even though I knew she wouldn't care that the Raptors beat the Knicks or the Leafs traded for Schneider, I could tell her anyway, like my sister talking about kids, husbands, and the washing machine backing up over the basement.

And even though I knew she wouldn't say, she was telling me about God, how He was for her, even how He would hold my hand if Bob happened to die before me. She knew I wanted us to go together, like a Ganges funeral pyre burning midnight over Trout Lake.

Flight Home

We come into this world alone and leave this world alone. The soul always travels alone.
—Reminder from an Indian Saint

At thirty thousand feet, breathing becomes fragile, suspended inside the metal handiwork of coffee-pumped engineers from Boeing, the moist fingers of earth ripped from my skin. I look down, seeking the feel of warm Indian Ocean rolling over my arms, palm trees muting the company of macaws squawking their hybrid mango-pine needle caw.

Or maybe I'll spot a young finch in the lone willow stirring my flat Iowa backyard, or black specks of Hondas and Cherokees cruising the Long Island expressway listening to Oldie Goldies.

Maybe I am still expecting the dirt road, clustered rooftops of Kanchipuram, its towering temple *gopuram* stacking figures of Hindu gods, *Lakshmi* and *Hanuman* reaching up to touch me, the smell of sandalwood working sweet lilacs through my Lufthansa-starch pores.

But I look out the airplane porthole and see only ice: North Atlantic stilled; white ghost trails abandoned on sheets of black holes, frozen, empty; ocean breath stopped, like a stone cemetery plotted black and white. Effigies startle naked.

Stripped land, stark white, drifts by my porthole eyes: crevicing dried-tongued snow I am hoping is a road, should be a road; mirage telephone poles; wind drifts that splinter like skidoo tracks, but are not.

Nothing moves except the plane, humming, shuddered, suspended. No trees stop the forgotten memory of wind, numbed below zero, my face, bitter white on white, bare to silence—so cold, so pure north bones wrenching me alone.

INDIA

Now that I've left my shoes at your door and bent my western body to touch your feet, will you enter my bones like the scent of sandalwood curling through the silent passages of my mind, or will you circumambulate my life like a temple ritual offering a flame to my outstretched hand?

I hear a thousand names of God burning the early morning darkness. Dispossessed of solitude, you wrap my mind in soft flesh, reaching through the noise like an invisible hand of silence, always present but never noticed, until I call Her name.

She was waiting for me like an offering left beside the road: India, the hand of a beggar extending not fingers but five mute stumps cut short by leprosy. Or was it sadistic despair that sliced them for a rupee?

The pleas of a vendor offer a necklace of red coral. Or is it red deceit? Eyes fixed in silent retreat could be the blessing of a true *sadhu*, or a beggar's rags dragged over the despondent.

You offer no black and white truth, only the possibility that maybe it is God talking to me through the scruffy beard of flies swarming around rancid sweat caked patiently over a sacred vow.

Mother *Ganga* roars silent ice into my frozen bones. Rameshvaram's ancient stones pour thousands of years of holy waters into the pores of my sins. You give your blessings, even to the beggar who cheats you, even to the man who smells of dung-stained feet.

Transcendental Transformer

To one of India's greatest sons

I have carried you with me for almost thirty years, or perhaps it is you that has been carrying me all this time. We arrived in India inseparable, what you taught me with meditation filtering everything I saw, like a blueprint sieving the truth from the mirage. This was the land of the Vedas, the total package of physical and metaphysical truth squeezed into my awareness, like a toothpaste tube with ingredients listed in English scientific, natural Sanskrit flavor added.

Like any noble truth seeker, I wanted what the ancient scripts and sages spoke of, the full electric current of enlightenment rushing through my awareness in a quantum awakening, my bare finger plugged into the live socket permanently.

The voltage in India is 220, way too much for western appliances. Like any wise teacher, you knew that, so you put your finger in the socket, stepped the current down to western 110 and held my hand. When I arrived in India, armed with my transformer kit, any Indian appliance was immediately usable. I could understand the truth emanating like silver sparks from a cosmic short circuit. I knew the hardware with the skill of an engineer sharing elegance in an uninterrupted flow of conceptions.

What I didn't know on first arriving in India was that the circuit had a life of its own, its own shape of God in the face of Mother. Her feet stir the dance of the *Tandava* rhythms of *Lord Shiva* released from the silence. Colors of red and gold, white and blue, wave through the current in a stream of consciousness and burn a flame of offering in my heart.

I look at the Vedic observatory you imprinted in my mind and sense the silent center of *Lord Shiva*, His solitude a *lingam* of perfect stillness. The red *bindu* of the *Sri Chakra*, Divine Mother, is the center of the cosmos in His heart. He dances to Her, and in His love, She releases the creation from destruction. The *Rig Veda* spins like a cosmic roulette wheel out from the silence.

Not just one divine figure, but every face of the divine, rises from the center of this vortex: the light of Christ, Guru Dev, circles of great *rishis* spilling outward, speaking the names of God. Each cognition is another segment in the wheel held together by the power of love: God and Mother, Goddess and Father, one graceful dance, flowing in the silence, bending my forehead, wanting to touch your feet.

Lessons from India

I did not know that my heart was held hostage by reason, that work, appointments, the ethic of social obligation could be flexible on a minute-to-minute basis, take second place to God. Before I met you, did I know that God could be happy, that I could forget the words in a prayer and not mind? Did I even conceive of God spilling out of His somber disguise of sin and retribution, atonement, and all forms of green puss oozing out of my personality?

How, after meditating for over twenty-five years, did I expect that I could keep God under lock and key trapped in my silent cave of blissful meditation, reserved for my "private" life? You told me I didn't have to forget Him when I went to work, didn't have to couch my words in the monotheism of money.

You even told me that He was She, and that beyond personification was only That, One formless Unbounded shaking free in a spectacle of light. Life's magical forms, the sinner and the saved, the loved and unloved, you and I, all are moving specimens of that silent light refracting through the density of hands and eyes, logical sequences induced with groins.

I always cherished Mother Nature, even more than the distant, male "God" I imagined was overseeing my life. She seemed so close at hand, fingers of white pine trees kneading my lungs, spirits of pungent oil penetrating my bones with cleansing inspiration. Fairways of green grass on green share the sunlight with morning dew, bathing my bare feet, showering my eyes, empowering each fragment of me with the velvet cohesion of being Her.

You gave Her form, detailed Her thousand faces, Her thousand hands, Her unrelenting nurture. You knew She was the power propelling the creation, fitting all the moving pieces of compelling distraction: Goddess, inseparable from God.

And without even trying, without either of us knowing, you handed Her to me, placed Her in the center of my heart, human love I could only imagine in Christ.

INDIA IN TRANSLATION

Inspired by quotes from Sri Karunamayi

Seva: service,
give, whatever your talents.
Bhakti: devotion,
"flow like a river, melt your humanness"
into the divine. A "new vibration" for your body,
bharati: self-effulgent light.

Every eye I glance at,
a story stilled.
Take the love Mother gives and pass it on.
Tyagi: "one who gives."

The Hindu newspaper reports Bihar's state assembly
is placed in suspended animation.
Private armies of landlords kill the landless,
warning, "Do not demand your right to land!"
Maybe the assembly will return from suspension
with a new body, a *bhakti* body.

I place my small personality in suspended animation
(*sadhana*: meditation)
and hope I'll return and give my land to the homeless.

Dale shaves his head,
works in Australia each year
just long enough to support his habit
of helping lepers in India.

Monica Lewinsky says the American president struggled
with his sexuality. He couldn't help
letting his hand glance against her breast.

"*Six enemies to liberation*:
anger, lust, greed,
jealousy, ignorance, pride."

Mother pours honey into the earth until it flows over.
Then She gives more.

The U.S. president sacked the Supreme Justice.
Hilary ran for New York.
Maybe suspended animation would be in order,
return with a new body.
"*Yogi*: one who has no desires."

Breasts are capable of feeding all the children of the world.
To be with Mother one must give.
Eradicate hunger. Suspend animation long enough
to feel the eye of God
searching for me in the dark,

listening for the sound
of the sacred bead
humming in the silence.

Epilogue

Experiences are events in the timeless, blips in the awareness. Maybe journeys are simply our minds connecting the dots. How we connect them is our own creation. Perhaps this is what is meant by *maya*, the mirage journey propelled by our interpretations, our comprehension limited or unlimited, depending on how cosmic the scale of our lens.

Ultimately, we never leave,
simply remember a larger Self.

Glossary

Note: With respect for the Indian tradition, spiritual terms and deities are listed separately from common words. Here, the common words are listed at the end of the glossary.

Meanings are simplified in many cases to reflect the intent expressed by the author, and are taken from dictionaries (indicated by *D)*, websites (*G* for Google, or *www..*), understandings learned from Maharishi Mahesh Yogi (*M*), or courtesy of the glossary in *Blessed Souls, The Teachings of Karunamayi, Volume One* (*B*).

Aarati: (B) Devotional waving of the flame of a ghee or oil lamp before a deity or holy person, accompanied by songs and offerings. The flame represents the light of Divine Consciousness, and the lamp, the individual soul seeking oneness with the Divine.

Ahimsa: Non-violence

Ashram: (B) Hermitage or retreat of a sage or *Guru*.

Asuras: (B) Demons in us, such as insatiable desire, anger, pride, hypocrisy, hardheartedness, harsh speech, delusion, ignorance of right conduct, and the inability to distinguish Self from action.

Avatar: (B) An incarnation of Divine Consciousness on earth who comes in an act of free will to protect the good, destroy evildoers, and reestablish righteousness.

Baba: (D) Father. Used also in names of male saints as a respectful yet familiar form of address. In this book *Baba* refers to the holy man, Sri Sathya Sai Baba, who is revered by millions worldwide as an avatar with miraculous powers. Cf: www.srisathyasai.org.in

Bharat:(B) India is known as Bharat or Bharata, in honor of King Bharata of the Lunar Dynasty, the brother of the great *Lord Ram* who was exiled for fourteen years. Bharata was so devoted to his brother that he refused to accept the throne himself and placed Lord Ram's sandals on the throne and ruled on his behalf.

In the spiritual meaning of the word, Maharishi Mahesh Yogi has stated that the root of Bharat means that which is real, that which is beyond the illusion or *maya* of the transitory material world. Sri

Karunamayi has referred to it as self-effulgent light.

Bhavani: (B) The one who creates or dispels illusion. The consort of *Lord Shiva* or *Bhava*.

Bindu: (B) Drop or spot. A symbol for the universe in its unmanifest form. The starting point from the void where all lines and forms may emerge. In the *Sri Chakra*, the *bindu* in the inmost triangle is the Abode of Bliss, or *Shiva-Shakti* in union, before manifestation.

Chandra: The moon. Also considered a divine being.

Chakra: (B) (wheel:circle) Centers of spiritual, subtle energy (kundalini) in the astral or subtle body of human beings. Of the many chakras in the body, seven are considered major, the six along the spine from the base to the forehead, and the seventh just above the crown of the head.

Chit: The mind.

Darshan: (B) To receive the blessing of a deity or holy person, by either seeing the auspicious form of that deity or holy person in consciousness, or by actually being in their physical presence. *Darshan* is the philosophy or angle of Truth which that deity or holy person imparts.

Dharma: (B) (dhri: to hold or retain) Righteousness or virtue; upholding the moral order.

Durga: (B) An aspect of one of the triune goddesses, *Parvati/Mahalakshmi Devi*. Consort of *Lord Shiva*. She manifested, seated upon a lion, to slay the demons of the mind. She is fearless and Her ten hands symbolize Her omnipotence.

Ekambareshwarar: A major temple in Kanchipuram in south India dedicated to *Lord Shiva*. It has a sacred mango tree reported to be 3500 years old; devotees wanting children pray to it.

Ganesh: (B) God of wisdom and remover of obstacles. Worshipped at the start of rituals or undertakings to bring success. Elephant-faced son of one of the triune Gods, *Lord Shiva* and His consort *Parvati Devi*.

Ganga Devi: Goddess of the holy Ganges River.

Gayatri: (B) The *Devi* or Goddess who protects. The wife of *Brahma*, one of the Hindu triune Gods, and the mother of the *Vedas* (Truth). Goddess of the Sun who presides over the *Gayatri* mantra, considered to be the most powerful and sacred mantra of the *Rig Veda*.

Gopuram: (D) Tall, pyramid-type tower abutting the entrance to a temple, especially in south India. Has intricate figures of Gods and Goddesses carved into the stonework.

Guru Dev: (B, M) *Guru*, teacher, one who leads the student from the darkness of ignorance to the light of True Knowledge. *Dev* means the one who shines, or the light of God. Guru Dev may refer to any guru, but here it specifically refers to Brahmananda Saraswati, guru of Maharishi Mahesh Yogi, and one of the most revered holy men of India. After forty years in solitude in the Himalayas, Guru Dev became the *Shankaracharya*, or spiritual leader, of Jyotir Math, one of the four major seats of Knowledge upholding the Vedic traditions of the ancient *rishis* (seers).

Hanuman: (B) Monkey chieftain who served *Lord Rama*. Personifies the ideal of service to a master and devotion to God.

Homa: (B) Ritual fire ceremony in which mantras are chanted, and offerings such as rice, honey, and lotus petals are made to express devotion and to ask for the blessings of a deity.

Japa: Practice of worship in which a mantra is repeated, using sacred beads as a counter.

Kama Sutra: (D) One of the Tantric texts related to the art of love.

Krishna: (B) *Lord Krishna* is the eighth incarnation, and best loved form, of *Vishnu*, one of the Hindu Triune Gods. He is worshipped as a Parnavatara, meaning that all other deities are considered to be His manifestations. He is also regarded as pure consciousness and the supreme yogi, statesman, warrior, and teacher. He is known for His clear exposition of the philosophic principles of Truth of the *Upanishad*, expressed in the *Bhagavad Gita* (Song of God).

Kumkum: (G) An auspicious red powder used in *pujas*, or the worship of deities. After offerings, it is placed as a red dot on the forehead of the worshipper.

Kunja Devi: (G) Female deity of a small mountainside temple in the Himalayas above Rishikesh that marks the place where the heart of Mother Divine landed.

Lakshmi: (B) Divine Mother in Her auspicious and sustaining form. Luminous Goddess of abundance, joy, and fortune, both material and spiritual. Consort of *Lord Vishnu*, one of the Triune Hindu Gods.

Lalitambika: (B) A loving form of address for Divine Mother in Her exquisite embodiment as *Lalita Devi*, who is the playful one, or the one responsible for the play of the universe. She manifested to destroy the demon Bhanda, who symbolizes the embodied soul, ignorant and egoistic, and identified solely with the body.

Lila Shakti: Cosmic energy (*shakti*) of the play (*lila*) of the universe.

Lingam: (B) A cylindrical-shaped symbol of *Lord Shiva,* made or naturally formed of stone or metal. Its form encompasses creation, movement, and absorption of the planets in Cosmic Energy (*shakti*). Likened to the Cosmic Egg of creation or to the flame of the Light of Consciousness. During worship, offerings of rice, honey, flour, etc. are poured over the *lingam* while the priests chant Vedic hymns.

Mahabharata: (G) The longest epic poem in the world, depicting the civil war in the time of the Kauravas and the Pandavas. The most important section is the *Bhagavad Gita,* which is a dialogue between *Lord Krishna* and the warrior leader Arjuna in which *Krishna* lays down the main precepts of the path of Truth. The *Gita* is considered to be the essence of all the Vedas.

Maharishi: (B) (*maha*, great + *rishi*, seer) A title given to a saint to indicate a great *rishi* (seer of Truth), or a reference to *Prajapati* ("Lord of Creatures," the progenitor or creator). *Brahma* is the first *Prajapati*, the active creator of the universe. His son, *Swayabhuva Manu* (mind-born man), created the seven *rishis* from whom mankind has descended. In this book Maharishi, when used alone, refers to Maharishi Mahesh Yogi.

Maharishi Mahesh Yogi: (1918-2008) The great holy man who founded Transcendental Meditation (TM) and popularized it around the world as a means to improve life on every level. TM's natural simplicity and Maharishi's use of scientific research to verify its results brought meditation out of the abstraction of mysticism into practical use as a tool for everyday living. His advanced TM-Sidhis program, and its practice in large groups to create harmony and coherence in national and world consciousness, are at the forefront of Maharishi's lifetime of dedication to revitalize the ancient Vedic knowledge (science of consciousness) in its purest form for the peace and wellbeing of all for generations to come. Cf: www.TM.org, also www.MUM.edu

Mala: (B) String of precious beads, or garland of flowers. Also a *stotra*, or garland of mantras.

Mandala: (D) (circle) A Hindu or Buddhist representation of the cosmos, characterized by a concentric configuration of geometric shapes, which contain an image or attribute of a deity.

Mangalyam: (G) (also *mangalsutra*) Sacred thread with pendants, worn by married women. Symbolizes love and dignity, and the auspicious opportunity to practice Right Religion. Considered to have divine power, protecting the marriage from evil and ignorance.

Maya: (D) Illusion, or ignorance of mistaking the material world for the reality.

Moksha: (D) Liberation. State of awareness freed from bondage and the attachment of delusion.

Mother Meera: (1960-) An embodiment of the Divine Feminine who gives silent *Darshan*, a spiritual blessing of love and light by touch and sight to thousands of people all over the world. This silent and non-denominational way to receive a new, transformative Divine Light (the *Paramataman* light) is free from any allegiance to a guru or organization, and is offered to help raise the consciousness of the world. Cf: www.mrreddy.org

Mudra: (B) A symbolic or ritual hand gesture or bodily posture that stimulates a specific cosmic energy in the individual and communicates a specific meaning.

Murti: (B) Image of a deity or holy person used for worship

Narayana: A name of *Lord Vishnu*, one of the Triune Hindu Gods.

Navaratri: (B) (*nava*, nine + *ratri*, night) The nine sacred nights dedicated to the worship of Divine Mother, the first three nights dedicated to *Durga*, the next three to *Laksmi*, and the last three to *Saraswati*. It is the celebration of the light of Divine Mother in the battle and victory over darkness (evil), and spiritually represents the struggle that each person has in balancing and overcoming the negative energies within. Navaratri happens four times a year but is mainly celebrated in the Spring and Fall, with the Fall Navartri considered the most important time of worship of Divine Mother. The tenth day, *Vijaydasami,* is the most auspicious day of victory over darkness.

Padmatavi: (G) The female deity in a south Indian temple in Tiruchanoor, near Tirupathi. The Great Divine Mother *(Adishakti),* who is the Ultimate Reality, the Supreme Power of God Almighty. The essence of unbounded Consciousness. Dwells in the *sahasrara* (crown *chakra*) of the individual and is the point of contact with Cosmic Consciousness.

Pallava: (G) Historical period (4th to 9th centuries) noted for its flourishing commerce and art, particularly the Shore Temple, the granite monolith, and the cave carvings of Mammallapuram.

Pradakshina: (D) Ritual circumambulation of a deity or holy place. In this book, refers to the circumambulation of the holy mountain Arunachala of *Lord Shiva*.

Puja: (B) Ritual worship of a deity, by chanting and making offerings (rice, honey, flowers, etc).

Pundit: (Skt *pandit*) Hindu priest versed in chanting the *Vedas* and performing Vedic rituals.

Punjabi: A type of lady's outfit (loose pants with a calf-length tunic). Named from dress typical of the people in the Punjab region of India.

Puranas: (D) Stories of Truth told in dialogues describing and celebrating the deeds of the Gods.

Rama (Ram): (B) Seventh incarnation of *Lord Vishnu*. Seen as the ideal son, king, husband, and warrior, because he willingly sacrificed his personal interests to the path of righteousness.

Ramakrishna: (1836-1886) One of the great spiritual geniuses of modern India. Practiced several spiritual disciplines, including Christianity and Islam, and concluded that all paths lead to the same One Reality. His famous disciple Swami Vivekananda brought *Advaita Vedanta* philosophy to the West. Cf: www.ramakrishna.org

Ramana Maharishi: (1879-1950) One of the greatest adepts of *jnana yoga* (yoga of knowledge) in the twentieth century. Noted for his self-inquiry ("Who am I?") approach to gain enlightenment, the discovery of the true Self beyond the physical body and the ego personality. His peaceful presence attracted thousands of seekers to his *ashram* in the sacred hill of Arunachala of *Lord Shiva* in Tiruvannamalai in south India. Cf: www.sriramanamaharishi.org

Ramayana: (B) Monumental epic poem depicting the high moral life of Lord Rama. Allegory for the battle within human beings between their better and worse selves.

Rig Veda: (B) The oldest, and longest of the four main branches of the Vedas, which are the foundation of complete knowledge of life passed on for thousands of years and still preserved in India. Oral hymns (later written) in praise of the powers of nature and natural law. Were cognized by enlightened sages or *rishis* who passed on these very specific Sanskrit sounds and the rituals and practices for a full life in tune with nature. *Rig Veda* details the knowledge of the process of creation and its functioning. (M) By just listening to these specific mantras, one is purified and elevated.

Rishi: A seer who cognized an aspect of the Truth and expressed it in a hymn of the *Veda*.

Rudraksha: (B) (*Rudra,* a name of *Lord Shiva* + *aksha*, eye) Sacred beads, commonly used in *japa malas* to count the number of repetitions of the *mantra* in the practice of worship. Seeds of a tree sacred to *Lord Shiva*, said to have originated from a tear shed from his eye for the sufferings of the world. (see note on *rudraksha* under *Sacred Beads).*

Sacred Beads: Here the author refers to sacred beads as symbolic of the mantras (seed sounds) used in meditation to allow for transcendence and the expansion of knowledge of the cosmic or universal Self at the basis of all life. These seed sounds are the vibrations that are fundamental to creation, and are embedded in the Sanskrit words of the Vedas chanted by the *pundits* in India.

Within this book also, the author makes reference to some types of beads worn for their spiritual value, or used as *japa malas* in the practice of worship. There is a body of knowledge about gems and their benefits specific to a person's astrological sign, but here the author refers in general to the spiritual value of some sacred beads. As described in www.karunamayi.org, "Sacred *malas* (garlands of beads) are made of auspicious substances that attract cosmic energy for peace, healing, abundance, divine love, and spiritual liberation."

Specific values or aspects are considered cultured by the type of beads used, e.g.:

"*Rudraksha* seeds…radiate tremendous life force…help to calm the mind, lower blood pressure, and fill (a person) with divine energy." Used by sages and yogis for thousands of years in India to "attract divine grace…and remove the many hurdles... in the spiritual path." Are "especially significant for practices related to *Lord Shiva*, like meditation."

Quartz crystal "emanates a transformative vibration of peace, purity and spiritual elevation…attracts the energy of *Saraswati Devi* for purity, education, higher awareness, and excellent spiritual growth…absorbs and transmits..divine energy into..each chakra (for it to blossom fully)…attracts the beneficial energy of Venus for love, serenity, and true harmony."

The *navaratna*, nine gems (or *navagraha*, nine planets) *mala* (like the *mala* on the front cover) "contains nine different gems which correspond to the nine planets of Jyotish or Vedic astrology. (Each) gem emits special vibrations which enter into (a person's) aura and creates a shield around (the person)… (This) will help deflect any negative energy from the planets and attract only the positive and auspicious energies….spiritual qualities will flower….and awareness of the Divine will expand."

Other types of beads mentioned by the author symbolized one aspect that could be cultured, i.e. red coral (strong heart), pink coral (mind and heart balanced), pearls (peacefulness).

Sadhu: (G) (virtuous one; straight, unerring) A holy man dedicated to the search for God. A *sadhu* may or may not be a yogi or a *sannyasin,* or be connected in any way with a guru or legitimate lineage. *Sadhus* usually have no fixed abode and travel, unattached, from place to place, often living on alms. There are countless *sadhus* on the roads, byways, mountains, riverbanks, and in the *ashrams* and caves of India. By their very existence they are said to have a profound, stabilizing effect on the consciousness of India and the world.

Samskaras: (B) Impressions or tendencies in an individual's consciousness that are the result of that individual's thoughts and actions in this life, as well as in previous births. The collection of a person's *samskaras* form that person's character.

Sanatana Dharma: (D) The path of eternal Truth or righteousness, passed on from the ancient Vedic seers or *rishis* of India.

Sannyasin: (G) One who, having fulfilled his family duties, turns to the spiritual path and dedicates his life to the spiritual growth of himself and those he teaches. In the Holy Order of *Sannyasa*, members don the saffron robes and take vows of renunciation and allegiance to God.

Saraswati: (B) Mother of Creation in the female Triad. Saraswati Devi bestows all knowledge, spiritual and secular. She reveals the path of Knowledge and is the origin of *nada* (primal sound) or the essence of all sound inherent in creation: speech, music, the voice of all nature, and the creative arts. She gives inspiration and mastery in the creative arts, and from Her all words and writing originated. Consort of *Brahma*, the Creator in the Hindu Triune God.

Satsang: (B) (in the company of Truth) Association with saintly people and listening to their teachings for purification and inspiration. A gathering of spiritual aspirants to chant, meditate, or discuss spiritual subjects.

Sesha: The serpent coiled as a bed for *Lord Vishnu* to rest upon.

Shakti: (D) (energy) The active manifest power that creates the universe. Consort of *Shiva*.

Shiva: (B) One of the divinities in the Hindu Triune God. Revered as God of Dissolution of the universe and of ignorance. He is in constant meditation and is considered the transcendental supreme consciousness. He is worshipped as the Absolute in the form of the *lingam*.

Shiva-Shakti: (B) The Tantric concept for the inseparable combination of spirit and matter, represented as male and female. In the state of *Samadhi* or balanced intellect, *Shiva-Shakti* unite in the *sahasrara chakra* (subtle energy center in the crown of the head). They reside in the innermost center of the *Sri Chakra* and are immanent in all creation.

Sri Chakra: (B) (divine circle or wheel) A diagrammatic representation (see pg 143) utilized in both mental and actual worship of *Devi* as Supreme Goddess and Mother of Creation. It represents the macrocosm (universe) and the microcosm (the individual self) as essentially different manifestations of the same Energy or *Shakti*. The *Sri Chakra* has nine enclosures and nine intersecting triangles. According to the Kaula school, the apexes of the four triangles pointing upward represent *Shiva* and the five downward-pointing triangles represent *Shakti*. The *bindu*, or spot in the center, signifies the union of *Shiva* and *Shakti* before the manifestation of creation, that is, the complete absence of duality.

"A Sri Chakra made of quartz crystal," like the one on the front cover, "constantly attracts the most auspicious cosmic vibrations," and "transmits these subtle cosmic rays to the person who touches, views, or worships (it)…purifies and sanctifies one's home." (www.karunamayi.org)

Sri Karunamayi: (1958-) (*karuna*, compassion + *mayi*, mother) A familiar name given to Bhagavati Sri Sri Sri Vijayeswari Devi, an embodiment of Divine Mother whose birth on the auspicious Hindu *Vijayadashami* Day (commemorating the victory of good over evil) was foretold by the saint Ramana Maharishi. Beloved for Her deep compassion and knowledge of ancient Vedic wisdom, she is dedicated to universal peace and the spiritual upliftment of humanity. She travels the world to provide spiritual nourishment and love to all, and offers non-denominational public programs and individual blessings to help each person achieve the highest states of spiritual illumination and human values on their chosen path. Cf: www.karunamayi.org

Sri Suktam: (B) Eloquent, poetic hymn of praise to the deity *Lakshmi*.

Tandava: (D) (violent dance) Vigorous dance by a male dancer. Of the many forms of *tandava*, the prototype is *Shiva's* dance of bliss, *ananda tandava*. *Tandav* is the manifest state of *Shiva*, whose dancing brings all into creation. When the dance stops, creation dissolves into Him.

Veda (Vedic): (B) (*vid*, to know) Eternal Knowledge. The eternal laws of Nature and the Creation in the form of hymns revealed as sound to the *rishis*, who passed them on orally. Each hymn bears the name of the *rishi* who cognized it, hence the *Vedas* are known as *Srutis*, "what was heard." The hymns were recorded in ancient holy books, which are the foundation of *Sanatana Dharma* and the Hindu religion. There are four main branches of the *Veda*: *Rig* (*jnana yoga*, knowledge), *Yagur* (*karma yoga*, action), *Sama* (*bhakti yoga*, devotion), and *Atharva* (synthesis of the three), as well as several subsidiary *Vedic* hymns. These sounds have been passed on orally for generations and are still chanted and maintained by the *Vedic pundits*.

(*M*) As summarized in *Thirty Years Around the World, Dawn of the Age of Enlightenment Volume One*: Maharishi Mahesh Yogi revealed that it is not the words, but the gaps (between the words), that constitute the reality of the *Veda*. His teachings revived the knowledge of the basis of the *Veda*, the transcendent gap, or the unmanifest underlying all of life and available within everyone's awareness, as the key to enlivening the whole or totality of the *Veda*, (much like watering the root of a tree gives nourishment to the whole tree). It is in the fully awake self-referral state of an individual's awareness, where the *Veda,* or eternal knowledge of life and the laws of nature, reside; the knower, the known, and the knowledge exist as a unified wholeness. In this wholeness (*samhita*), the organizing power of nature (*brahmana*) emerges, and the whole creation unfolds. The gaps between the syllables, words, and verses of the *Veda* display this self-referral state of pure knowledge or wholeness. Maharishi described the *Veda* as pure knowledge (wholeness) and its infinite organizing power.

Venkateshwara: (G) The Lord who destroys the sins of the people. Presiding deity of the Tirupathi Tirumala Temple in south India. Known as *Venkatachalapathy*, *Srinivasa*, and *Balaji*, *Venkateshwara* is considered the supreme form of the Triune God *Vishnu*, incarnated in this age for the salvation and upliftment of humanity

Vijayeswari: (B) The Goddess of Victory who on the tenth day after Navaratri defeated the demons Chanda and Munda. Her victory commemorates the victory of good over evil and is one of the most auspicious days in the Hindu calendar.

Vishnu: (B) (*vis*, to pervade) One of the Triune Gods. Embodies *sattva*

guna, purity, peace, & goodness. Preserving Power of the Universe, Self-existing, All-pervading. His consort is *Lakshmi.*

Yamuna: (B) A sacred river near Brindavan, the location of many of *Lord Krishna's* childhood episodes and His cosmic dance with the milkmaids.

Yogi: One who is united with God.

Yogini: Feminine form of the masculine *yogi*. Possesses steadfast transcendence.

GLOSSARY OF COMMON WORDS

Chapati: A type of Indian flatbread

Dahl: A type of soupy, spiced legume or bean

Dhanyavad: Hindi word for thank you

Dhoti: (D) A traditional long loincloth worn by Hindu men, especially during times of worship

Ghee: Clarified butter used for worship (in lamps) and for cooking

Lungi: (D) Everyday waist-wrap of silk or cotton, worn by Indian men, especially in South India

Pakora: A snack of fried batter with vegetable or fruit inside

Pan: (D) A leaf of the betal vine chewed in parts of India

Roti: A type of Indian flatbread

Wala: (D) Hindi/Urdu word for a seller or vendor, e.g., a *chai wala* (one who sells tea)

Parting Notes to the Traveler

Tips for Traveling Minus Five Star India

Carry toilet paper in your pocket, always. Sling a daypack on your back and never leave your hotel without it.

Essential items in the daypack? Water in a flip-top bottle you lugged from America, the prize spout as rare in India as toilet paper.
Pocket flashlight. You wonder why? After all, you are not planning a camping trip.

In India every day is an outdoor adventure, streets with no street lights, black as curfew when the equatorial sun plummets out of existence at six p.m. and leaves you wondering where the next drop of dog doo awaits your freshly bare sandaled toes. Or is it your pleasure to haunt the cracks in the sidewalks that are ankle wide and deep enough for you and the garbage, blue plastic, mango rot, and other unidentifiable remnants scoured by the earthworms.

Camping is possible even indoors in India, power failures a regular event programmed into the electrical circuits, bare wires slumped over the poles where the last crew supposedly repaired the blackout. Whip out your flashlight, and menus are transformed into readable items once again, giving you the edge on the other patrons waiting for the portable transformer to kick in with the decorous flair of a hippo charging a semi-trailer.

Or you may light your way back to bed, book in one hand, flashlight in the other, re-living your childhood, reading secretly way past even your parents' bedtime.

Street maps are useless, so don't bother to try to find one. The rickshaw drivers can't read them, and you can't either. There are no street signs.

The daypack is no place for your passport or your credit card. Secure them in a money belt, with loose change in your pocket for beggars and rickshaws.

If you were lucky and brought trail snacks from the U.S., you'll find them useful when hunger Richter scales the stomach crevices with nothing in sight but greasy *rotis* and unidentifiable mush frying three feet from the dogs and cows. As time passes, they appear more like hotdogs served by the licensed, hygienically stamped vendor you used to see at the Blue Jays/Red Sox game, until an hour after the dogs, and you are running, literally, to a western-trained M.D. you hope you can rely on.

If you forgot the snacks, and the hotdog *pakora* is almost to your mouth, stop. Go to the corner vendor. Buy crackers or biscuits, even if the package looks dusted from years haunting a roof-high shelf. There's a lot of soot and sand in India, and few vendors with feather dusters, so the box may not have waited for you that long.

Lonely Planet is THE guidebook for first timers and veterans, a blue trunk weighing in at three pounds, guaranteed to challenge you aerobically as it bumps up and down in the bottom of your pack. But you will need it, often at first, then occasionally, but always when you opted not to pack it.

Wear old clothes you don't mind being mangled into a new incarnation by the five-cent-a-shirt laundry: whites deconstructed into shamrock gray or pink blue; mediums re-channeled into large with pocks left from drying on the rocks.

Ear plugs. Don't forget them! You have never heard loudspeaker's cosmic capacity until you find your hotel across the street from a Hindu temple's three a.m. electronic blast of God's names delivered megahertz beyond any human range.

And always remember the toilet paper.
Oh, for a seat on a western porcelain goddess!

Wish for the Fellow Traveler

In the rugged night of your soul,
may you hear the sound of the sacred beads
like a rumor stirring the midnight air.

She is singing to you,
calling your name,
smoothing the chalice of silver and gold
lining your awakening.

Reach out to Her,
take Her hand,
let Her cradle you in Her arms.

Cry with Her
all the unborn tears that sheltered you
from your own joy.

Sing with Her
the lullaby of your childhood
that you can no longer forget.

And in that instant of your togetherness,
you will feel the silence.
You will know
where the sound comes from.

Then is your journey your own,
the night wind is your friend,
and the drops of rain are the guide for your footsteps,
melting your heart,
holding you home.

About the Author

Susan Klauber was born and raised in the Northern Ontario mining hub of Sudbury, Canada, and has lived and traveled in Europe, North and South America, and India. Married to an American, she currently spends her retirement time in Fairfield, Iowa, where she writes poetry and pursues her interest in spiritual development to create peace and uplift the collective consciousness.

Sound of the Sacred Beads: A Poet's Journey into India is her second book of poetry and prose. Based on eight winters of living and traveling in India, it draws upon the author's many years of experience with Transcendental Meditation to explore the inner realm of India and its impact on her life. She feels poetry and India are natural partners that lead individuals into a common spiritual core, where the most profound knowledge and experience of life occur.

Her poetry and prose have appeared in the Harcourt Canada textbook *Elements of English 11,* in the journals *The MacGuffin, Poetry Motel, The Iowa Source, Contemporary Review*, and in the anthologies *Eclipsed Moon Coins: Twenty-Six Visionary Poets* and *The Dryland Fish.* Blue Light Press of Fairfield, Iowa published her first book of poetry and prose, *Face-off at Center Ice.*

Prompted by age or wisdom, she is now making the transition from ardent to occasional golfer and used-to-be hockey player.

To Contact the Author:

If you would like to share your comments on the book, or enquire about interviews or readings, please email the author at sandtrovepress@gmail.com